KAFUE ... ARK

Zambia

Peter de Vere Moss

Sponsored by:

Royal Danish Embassy
Zambia

Published by:

KAFUE TRUST

Acknowledgements

Firstly, the Trustees of the Kafue Trust and the author express their sincere thanks to the Royal Danish Embassy for their unstinting support and the confidence they have had in production of this first guide to Kafue National Park.

Our thanks are due to all members of the Zambia Wildlife Authority (ZAWA), members of the Kafue Park Operators' Association and to the many friends and colleagues who have enthusiastically contributed to the book, namely Andy Anderson, Jill Annfield, Arthur Ansell (mammals), Dr Stephen Berwick, Mike Bingham (vegetation), Igor Boltar, Michael Brett (mapping), Don Broadley (reptiles and amphibians), Jeremy Burnham, Judy Carr, Dr Harry Chabwela, Wilbroad Chansa, Rose Chivumba, Jack Chulu, Ken Coe, Chris Cooke, Julien De Groote, Bob Douthwaite, Tom and Vivienne Heinecken, Fred Hengeveld, Errol Hickey, Philip Jeffery, Richard Jeffery, Jacob Jepsen, Michael Kaingu M.P., Robin Lines (carnivores), Sitali Liwena, Dr Ian Manning, Litumelo Mate, Edwin Matokwani, Chris and Charlotte McBride, Tyrone McKeith, James Milanzi (ZAWA KNP management), Dr Francis Mkanda, Dean Morton, Tim Mushibwe, Kaj Øestergaard, Tony Pass, Yusuf Patel, Jean Michel Pavy, Donald Pelekamoyo, Sipho Phiri, Belinda Pumfrett, Dr Patrick Rogers, Dr Lewis Saiwana, Dr Victor Siamudaala, the late Bob Stjernstedt (birds), Corjan van der Jagt, Charles van Rensburg, Darrell Watt, Tom Younger and Dr Geoffrey Zyambo.

Thanks also to all other friends and colleagues who have helped so much in their different ways to bring this guidebook to the hands of everyone who loves the Park and to those who are interested in Zambia and its wonderful natural landscapes, wildlife and cultural heritage.

Very special thanks to Ambassador Thomas Schjerbeck for all his encouragement; to Dr John Hanks for immensely important technical contributions and meticulous editing of the text; to Michael Brett for preparation of all the maps; to Sarah Rachmann for design and layout; and to Professor Ian Swingland for his backing from the outset, support and guidance throughout and above all to Steve Smith to whom we are particularly indebted for his wholehearted and selfless commitment to the management of the entire production process.

The Kafue Trust

The Kafue Trust is an English charity registered in 1997 to support development of Kafue National Park and the communities residing in the surrounding Game Management Areas. The Trust owes its origin to the commitment of Graham Younger, who prior to his untimely passing away in 1997, was working with like-minded conservationists to establish a non-profit organisation to promote wildlife conservation and to facilitate training and research in and around Kafue. After Graham's sad demise his sons Tom and Mark helped publicise the Trust so that its objectives could be achieved mainly through a volunteer group working towards realising Graham's dream.

The Trust's aim is to provide professional assistance for park management, wildlife research and training for natural resource conservation, as well as to foster development of sustainable livelihood enterprises in the local communities.

Trust projects have included contributing to protection of the Ngoma Forest and to improving entrance gates and road signage. Plans are afoot now for a Master Action Plan in partnership with the Zambia Wildlife Authority (ZAWA) that will embrace further contribution to vital road infrastructure, biodiversity conservation, management of bush fires, tourism and economic empowerment programmes by placing people at the centre of development.

The Trust organised publication of this Visitor's Guide as a project in its own right in order to fill the information gap so that the Park can become better known and to encourage responsible tourism. We hope the book will help Kafue on its way forward as one of Zambia's great national assets. Kafue Trust's vision is for Kafue to take its rightful place as a world-class National Park of inestimable global value for present and future generations.

PUBLISHED AND DISTRIBUTED BY THE KAFUE TRUST

Email: *info@kafuetrust.org*
www.kafuetrust.org

Mapping by Michael Brett

Editing by John Hanks
Design and layout work by Sarah Rachmann

Cover photograph of sable herd by Dana Allen
ISBN 978-9982-22-459-8
First published 2013
Printed and bound by Future Publishing (Pty) Ltd

PHOTO ACKNOWLEDGEMENTS

(t denotes top of page, m denotes middle of page and b denotes bottom of page)

Andrea Porro 24m, 35m, 36m, 37m, 39t, 45, 114m, 114b **Austin Wienand/KRC** 76t, 76m **Belinda Pumfrett** 69b **Brian McMorrow** 78b, 79t, 135b **Caitlin Smith** 110m, 110b **Dana Allen/Wilderness Safaris** 1, 16t, 24t, 35t, 37t, 37b, 38t, 39m, 39b, 40b, 44t, 47, 88t, 88b, 128b **Darrell Watt** 80m **David Rattray/Wilderness Safaris** 143 **Dennis Bolton** 72b **Dottie Shober/GRI** 108t **Doug Reynolds/Royal Zambezi Wildlife** 78t, 78m **Edjan Van De Heide** 94m, 94b, 99t **Egbert De Kwaasteniet** 4t, 23b, 96b, 103m, 103b, 104t **Gilmour Dickson** 20t, 36t, 90b, 91m, 91b, 92t **Heinz Lambert** 21t **Ian Manning** 5b, 29t **Igor Boltar** 67b 75m, **Joe Hadley** 93m, 93b **John Hanks** 7t, 8b, 12t, 18b, 24b, 26b, 27m, 28t, 31m, 32t, 33b, 109m, 122b, 126b **Kenneth Coe** 26m, 27b, 28m, 28b, 29b, 31t, 60b **Ken Ferguson** 30b **Leopard Lodge** 34m, 50b, 77t, 77m **Mayukuyuku/Kafue Camps** 25m, 70b, 71m, 71b, 120b **Michael Poliza/Wilderness Safaris** 119t **Paul Changuion** 13b, 115b **Peace Parks Foundation KAZA TFCA** map **Peter Moss** 6t, 6b, 9t, 9b, 10b, 16b, 17b, 18t, 19t, 19m, 20b, 22t, 25b, 35b, 43t, 46b, 48t, 48b, 51t, 53t, 54t, 55t, 72t, 73m, 73b, 75t, 75b, 80b, 81m, 81b, 82b, 86t, 86b, 87t, 87b, 89t, 92b, 93t, 99m, 99b, 100b, 101t, 101m, 101b, 102m, 102b, 109b, 111b, 112m, 112b, 113m, 113b, 116b, 124b, 127t, 128t, 131, 133t, 136b, 139t, 144b, 145t, 167b, 169b **Robin Lines** 34t **Roger de la Harpe** 30t **Rhet A. Bulter/mongabay.com** 30m **Sergio Segura** 116t, 116m **Stephen Robinson** 31b, 65, 80t, 97b, 183b **South African Institute for Aquatic Diversity** 42t **Steve Smith** 15b, 23t, 27t, 32b, 41b, 50t, 54b, 58t, 59b, 87m, 115t, 115m, 117, 173b **Tom Heinecken** 95b **Tim Ivins** 25t **Tony Pass** 95t **Tyrone McKeith** 40t **Wilderness Safaris** 26t, 33t, 34b, 36b, 38m, 38b, 41t, 56b, 58b, 88m, 118m, 121t, 124t, 125t, 151t **Woody Cotterill** 147b

Contents

1. INTRODUCTION TO THE KAFUE NATIONAL PARK

Location and landscapes	3
History	5
Local communities	8
Geology and soils	10
Vegetation types	15
Wildlife	20
Climate	43

2. PLANNING YOUR TRIP

Special attractions of the KNP	48
How to get there	
Roads, entrance gates and charges, airstrips	52
Where to stay	59

3. WHERE TO GO AND WHAT TO SEE AND DO

North-East Area	67
North-West Area	83
Central Area	95
Southern Area	105

4. MANAGING THE KAFUE NATIONAL PARK

Why management is necessary	120
Management zones	123
Fire and firebreaks	125
Research and monitoring	128
Opportunities for Transfrontier conservation	129

5. TRAVEL TIPS

Visas and entry permits	132
KNP rules and regulations	133
Health and safety	134
Food and equipment	136
Banking and currency	138
Bookings, enquiries and useful contacts	139
Additional reading	142

6. WILDLIFE AND COMMON TREES

Large mammals	145
Small mammals	148
Birds	151
Common trees	168
Reptiles	170
Amphibians	172
Fishes	174
Local names of more common animals	176
Notes on common trees	177
Local names of common trees	184

MAPS

Access	Inside front
KNP and GMAs	2
Geology	11
Vegetation	14
North-East Area	68
North-West Area	84
Central Area	98
Southern Area	106
KAZA TFCA	130
Visitor accommodation	Inside back

INDEX 185

INTRODUCTION TO THE KAFUE NATIONAL PARK

The Kafue National Park (or KNP as the locals call it) is one of Africa's best kept secrets. An unspoilt wilderness with an outstanding variety of wildlife, it embraces a rich blend of woodlands, grasslands and aquatic environments in an extravagant celebration of complexity of shapes, colours, adaptations and interrelationships. Larger than the well-known Kruger National Park in South Africa, it covers 22,480 km^2 (8,650 square miles), representing 36% of Zambia's National Park land. Surrounded almost entirely by Game Management Areas, which cover a further 45,406 km^2, the combined total of wildlife estate is 68,000 km^2, twice the size of Belgium, an enormous national asset of over 9% of Zambia's entire land. Most of the Park lies at about 1,068 metres (3,500 feet) above sea level, in a zone of moderate rainfall, moderate temperatures and low humidity. It is a land without fences and few roads, much of it still remaining uncharted territory for the tourist.

Kafue National Park and Game Management Areas.

ZAMBIA

Landlocked Zambia is surrounded by eight countries located on the Central African Plateau, immediately south of the DRC, formerly Zaire. It has an area of 752,600 km² (290,578 square miles) with a population of about 13 million. The economy is based on mining, agriculture and a growing tourist industry, which mainly depends upon scenic attractions such as the Victoria Falls, wildlife in 19 National Parks and a marvellous variety of safaris. Zambia has many rivers, beautiful waterfalls, huge lakes, savanna woodlands, forests and floodplains intersected by deep valleys and steep escarpments.

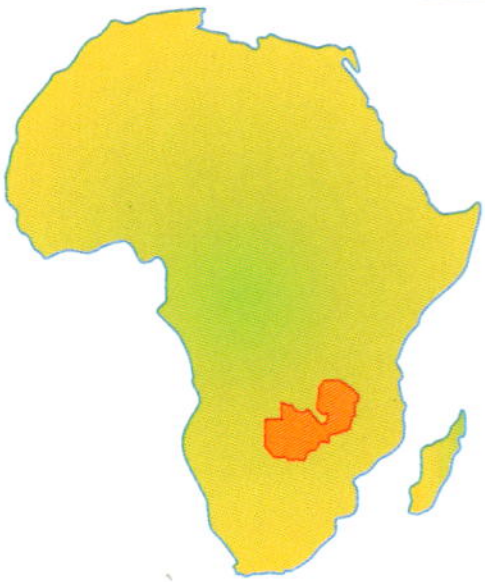

Republic of Zambia in southern Africa.

But it is KNP's extraordinary diversity which places it in a special category of its own. There are 160 species of mammals, with more antelope species (21) than any other park in Africa. Nowhere else in the continent can you see blue duiker, sable and roan antelopes, red lechwe, Lichtenstein's hartebeest, elephant, buffalo, lion, leopard, wild dog, hippo and if you are very lucky, yellow-backed duiker all in one Park. KNP is also the home of the wattled crane, crested guinea-fowl, black-cheeked lovebird, slaty egret, and nearly 500 additional species that make the Park one of Zambia's "Important Bird Areas", and a priority destination for enthusiastic birders.

After several lean years of insufficient resources for conservation and maintenance, the infrastructure and wildlife are recovering through financial support from the Royal Norwegian Embassy, the Royal Danish Embassy, UNDP, the World Bank and other international donors. This has led to invigorated management by the Zambia Wildlife Authority (ZAWA), which is encouraged and supported by a growing number of private lodge owners and the Kafue Trust. Derelict buildings are being restored, roads are improving (there are 2,600 km in KNP), poaching is declining and new lodges and camps are being constructed along the roads from north to south. The big herds of buffalo that used to roam everywhere and which made the Park famous are coming back and the prides of lion are following. Elephant are on the increase with breeding herds being seen frequently, and large herds of roan antelope (recently seriously diminished in numbers) are now being regularly recorded in places where they were scarce, such as along the remote western boundary on the line of the watershed between the Zambezi River to the west, and the Kafue River to the east.

LOCATION AND LANDSCAPES

KNP is located in western Zambia between S14°003' and S16°043' and E25°013' and E26°046', taking its name from the Kafue River that

Zambia and
any comments you may
have on the publication.

Please address such comments to The Publisher and email to pdevmoss@yahoo.co.uk

KA001

is the largest tributary of the Zambezi. The Park's wide landscapes are shaped by the Kafue River and the surface geology, dividing the major landscapes into the four natural areas, namely (i) North-East, (ii) North-West, (iii) Central, and (iv) Southern, conveniently grouping KNP's attractions into these areas, which form the essence of this Guide Book. The river itself dominates the numerous habitats and stretches through the Park for over 256 km, and is the core of KNP's drainage system with its right bank tributaries, aided by a few lesser tributaries to the north-east flowing to the left bank. The 14 principal rivers are named and shown on the main map and where they occur on the smaller section maps. With the exception of the Lunga and the Kafue itself, all of them cease to flow during the dry season. Pools remain in the seasonal rivers and these provide well-dispersed sources of water throughout the Park.

Apart from a few areas of low, well-weathered granite and sandstone hills, the landscape is gently undulating, with the highest point being Mutumbwe Hill at 1,478 metres (4,851 feet) in the north-east S14°49'48" E26°35'24", about 20 km south-west of Kabulushi Gate. The floodplains to the north and south and the riverine alluvial terraces are low-lying and relatively level.

Outstanding landscape features that make the KNP as a whole so special include:

- stretches of the Kafue River in the north-east

The Kafue River changes its mood from calm expanses and wide floodplains to swiftly flowing rapids between islands with dense forest patches, palm fringed lagoons, sand banks and rocky shores.

where its mood changes quickly between calm expanses and wide floodplains to swiftly flowing narrows between islands down to the Mwengwa Rapids, with dense forest patches of riparian woodland along much of its length;

· the Busanga Plain to the north-west, divided by several lesser tributaries;

· the widespread miombo and mopane woodlands, teak forest and patches of thickets;

· dambo grasslands, which are such a prominent feature of the Central African Plateau and which provide some superb wildlife photography opportunities;

· the rounded granite hills of Lubalanzuki and Kaindabaila Range in the central part;

· Lake Itezhi-Tezhi for boating and fishing; and the incomparable Nanzhila Plains in the far south.

HISTORY

The notion that wildlife, or "game" as it is often called, should be protected in the area of what is today the KNP dates back to the early nineteen twenties, more or less at the time that Northern Rhodesia was becoming a British Protectorate. It was already realised that wildlife was being randomly depleted and that steps should be taken to halt, maybe even to reverse that process. Len Vaughan, the first Game Ranger who began construction of the Park's infrastructure, commented in 1950 that there was a remarkable lack of "game" in many places, but in 1954 reported a steady recovery: *"Game continues to respond encouragingly to protection and is now beginning to show up in areas where it was previously almost non-existent. Added control by enforcement of park regulations has been exercised north of the Musa River and results have become evident in the appearance of small herds of game"*.

Senior Game Ranger Len Vaughan, first officer who started protection and development of KNP in 1950.

The first move was the formation of the Kafue Game Reserve that covered most of the northern part of the present National Park in line with the 1933 International Convention on the Protection of Flora and Fauna. From then, development of the idea that wildlife and wilderness areas should be conserved through protected areas took place actively over the pre-Second World War years, spanning the time up to about 1948 when discussions formally took place with the Provincial Administration and the Department of Game and Tsetse Control to expand the Game Reserve to include what is now all the land that lies within the southern sector.

These negotiations culminated in formation of the Kafue National Park that was proclaimed on 20 April 1950. The main purpose was to safeguard a large part of the Kafue River's western catchment that included an area in the centre and south-west known as the Cordon Controlled Area. The Cordon was a simple bush road built originally in the 1930s as a patrolled line constructed to prevent cattle from western areas of Barotseland/the Western Province from carrying pleuropneumonia to emerging commercial ranches and traditional cattle keeping country of the Ila tribe to the east.

After much debate, the western boundary was finally delineated in 1956, closely following much of the Kafue/Zambezi watershed for almost 300 km from Kasempa District in the north to Kalomo District in the far south. To the east, the River forms about 150 km of the boundary down to Itezhi-Tezhi Dam, after which it traverses the western side of the Kafue Flats passing southwards to the Dundumwezi Entrance.

Following creation of the National Park, it was accepted that the conservation rules that would apply within the Park boundary would be introduced less rigorously in the surrounding Chiefs' tribal areas where residence and controlled hunting would be permitted. Most of these were to become the

Above: Frank Ansell was Warden of the KNP in the late 1960s, continuing his outstanding work on documenting the mammals of Zambia.

Below: Wildlife Scout Eitone Siyanga looking down on the Musa River and Puku Flats before Lake Itezhi-Tezhi impoundment.

Kalala Island Camp in 1968 before it was flooded by Itezhi-Tezhi dam.

present-day Game Management Areas that provide a lower level of wildlife protection, acting as corridors and buffers to the Park, which would thus become a well-protected core area within which hunting, agriculture and residence would not be allowed.

In the early years visitor accommodation was being gradually constructed and by 1957 tourist camps were functioning at Ngoma, Nanzhila, Kalala, Itumbi, Chunga, Mapunga, Lufupa, Mosi, Treetops, Lushimba and Ndulumina, all of which were run by the Game Department. Ngoma lodge was the only fully catering facility and this was completed in 1958, in time for the official opening of the Park by the Governor General of that time. Of these camps only four, Nanzhila, Treetops, Kafwala and Lufupa, remain operational.

A significant change to the landscape occurred in 1977, when the Itezhi-Tezhi Dam construction was completed and water reached its highest water level. Lake Itezhi-Tezhi cut through the main north / south road in the KNP and submerged forever Kalala Island camp and Puku Flats renowned for its superb wildlife viewing.

LOCAL COMMUNITIES

The Park is known for its size and its abundance of wildlife species, but unfortunately local people are often overlooked. Thus information has been included about the people who once resided here for hundreds, maybe even thousands of years. People are very much part of the Park's history, ecology and the shaping of its ecosystem. The original inhabitants moved out when KNP was formed, but to this day some still enter the Park every year at the end of the rains to harvest fish using the same methods they have used since time immemorial. As you will find in these pages, the people played a major role in how the landscape, wildlife and vegetation in particular have evolved and how and why species occur where they do.

The impact of man on the environment continues through development of tourism and through poaching and annual burning of the bush. Outside the Park, in the Game Management Areas, expansion of agriculture and extraction of timber and charcoal and unsustainable hunting and fishing, are causing depletion of forest cover and natural resources in general. When the Park was formed the government arranged for the resident villages to relocate outside the Park boundary since it was no longer legal to live within its boundaries. Some of the villagers negotiated rights to continue to harvest fish, honey, grass and other forest products that they had always harvested seasonally to coincide with the flowering of plants and the times of the year when rivers start to flow. Agreements negotiated with the Provincial Administration and Game Department of the time recorded how they would be allowed to use these "Usufruct Rights".

COMMUNITIES ADJACENT TO THE KNP

- Busanga Fishermen from Kasonso and Kasempa.
- Villages of Kabulwebulwe near the Kafue Hook.
- Kaingu villages – the middle Kafue.
- Nanzhila fishermen from Shezongo.
- Hunter-gatherers from Katinti north of the Musa River.

Local communities living close to the KNP still continue with their traditional way of life.

These agreements still stand and visitors are able to witness some of the traditional activities and learn about this ancient part of local culture that continues to the present day. The main difficulty at the moment is access in the rainy season when the traditional fishing takes place, and until the Park has more all-weather roads, reaching the sites on the Busanga Plain in the north and on the Nanzhila River in the south is a major 4x4 expedition that will require a great deal of careful planning, although much depends upon how long the rains last and how much flooding occurs.

With growing interest in the National Park and with the Government's plans for development of infrastructure and strengthening management, a study of the five groups of villages that were dispossessed of their land and, to a large extent, their livelihoods, could be of great value in understanding the ecology of this kind of fish harvesting. In addition, both the environment and local communities could benefit from better management and even integration into tourism to some extent.

Above: Traditional fisherfolk working a weir on the Nanzhila River.

Below: Ila pastoralists herding their cattle.

Principles of helping local communities to become more involved in management and to become owners of natural resources are now well understood and successfully used in many places in East and southern Africa. Participation of communities in planning and management is today accepted as the first step to sharing the rewards of improved natural resource management and eventually for achieving higher returns from sustainable natural harvests.

The Ila, Tonga, Kaonde and Lozi communities walked through the forests, along the rivers and across the plains of what is the KNP of today, hunting, gathering and later building fish traps and weirs, and then starting to grow crops and keeping cattle. They were well-adapted to the changing of the seasons, of tsetse infestations, marauding animals and use of fire. They were the first to know the mysteries of the hills, the caves, the hot springs, the swamps and the vistas of Kafue. The descendants of these people still live around the Park and it is hoped that they will recognise its value and derive greater benefits than in the past from the development of tourism and other enterprises based on wild resources.

Below: Sedimentary rocks at the centre of Longola hot springs at the western edge of the Kafue Flats.

GEOLOGY AND SOILS

This brief outline of the geology of the Park is based on the work of the geologist J.G. Simpson, which he carried out in 1967. It is, of course, the geology of an area that is the basis of the physical foundation to the total ecology of the KNP and is at the core of the wonderfully diverse ecosystem. The KNP is a great place to see at first hand some of the fascinating ancient geological formations, which

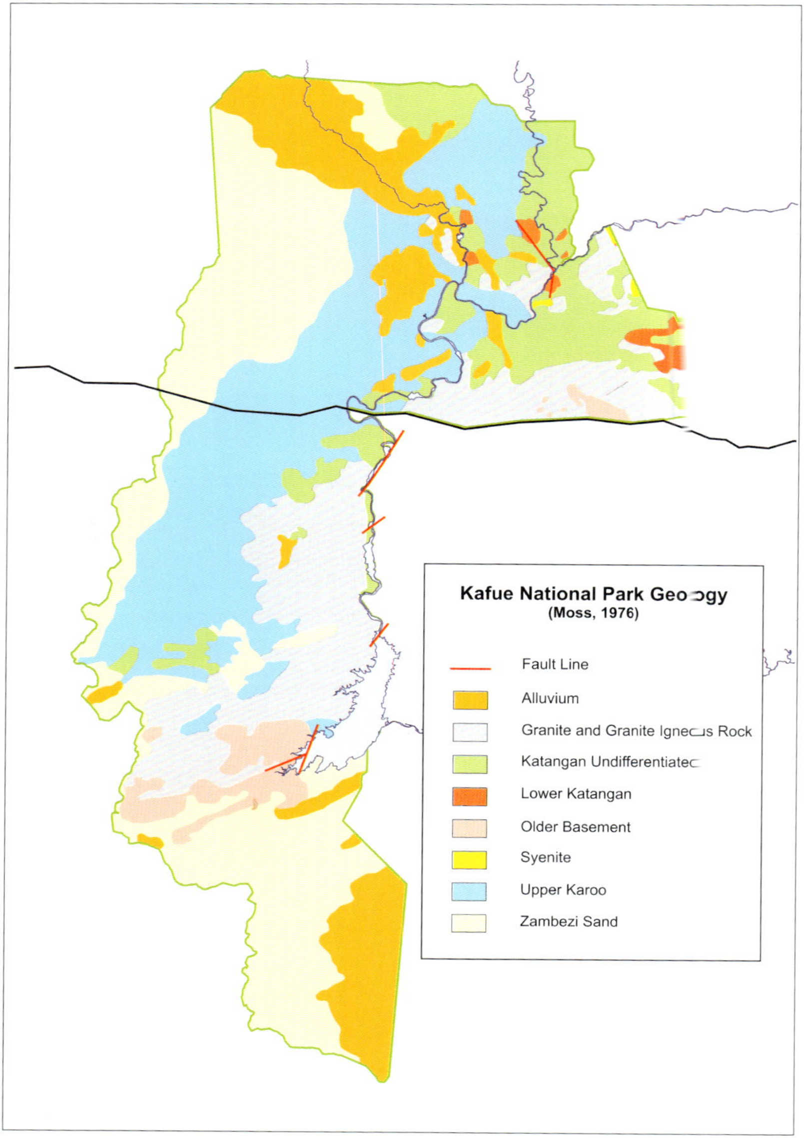
Kafue National Park Geo ogy
(Moss, 1976)
Fault Line
Alluvium
Granite and Granite Igne us Rock
Katangan Undifferentiate
Lower Katangan
Older Basement
Syenite
Upper Karoo
Zambezi Sand

Granite ridge overlooking the Musa River floodplain before Itezhi-Tezhi dam was inundated.

are among the oldest in the world. The rocks that form the surface geology of the Park include very ancient Precambrian basement granite, granite-gneiss and schist; later Pre-Cambrian quartzite, slate, grit and limestone of the Katanga system; Karroo sandstone and shale and the very young Zambezi sands. The map on page 11 will show you where there are outcrops of hard granite rocks and in other places where alluvial soils predominate indicating how some rocks have withstood erosion over millions of years. The alluvial sediments occur over the entire Busanga Plain and in patches further south near the Kafue Hook, and then in narrow belts along the lower Musa and Nkala Rivers and in a broad zone 8 to 16 km wide along the south-eastern boundary.

The central portion of KNP is occupied by the south-western extension of the Hook granite massif. Exposed elements include high grade schist and gneiss, granite-gneiss and granite, with the granite forming typical tor of strongly resistant rocky outcrops and as seen in the numerous rapids in the Kafue River between Itezhi-Tezhi and Chunga, a wonderful place to go for some dramatic landscape and river photography, as are the granite hills at Lubalanzuki and Kaindabaila. Rocks of the Katanga system are found on the margins of the granite massif and consist of little metamorphosed slates, quartzites and limestones that were originally sediments in large bodies of water. The history of the Zambezi sands, which form deposits along the western boundary and the southern quarter west of the alluvial plains, is still a subject for controversy, but it seems probable that their origins are both lacustrine (formed at the bottom of a lake) and aeolian (wind-blown). These immense sands were previously called Kalahari and later Barotse loose sands.

All soils initially come from rocks, known as the 'parent material', and these may be directly below the soil or some distance away and brought there by a combination of wind and water. The formation of soils is termed 'pedogenesis', a complex interaction between the geology and local climate that has led to the formation of the diversity of the soils and their characteristics that support the Park's major plant communities and their related animal associations. Pedogenesis is an on-going process of which a further key part is the organic decomposition made possible by the soil's micro-organisms, and this will be further shaped by the material that accumulates in any one area as plants and animals die. The details of the soil types found in the Park are beyond the scope of a visitor's guide. What is important to note, however, is that the plant communities you will see as you travel through KNP will be linked to soil composition and characteristics, and then further influenced over time by a host of additional modifying factors such as micro-habitats, slope, the effects of past land use (particularly agriculture), flooding regimes and drainage, and the effects of fire.

Mopane woodland in the autumn - southern area near Kalenje.

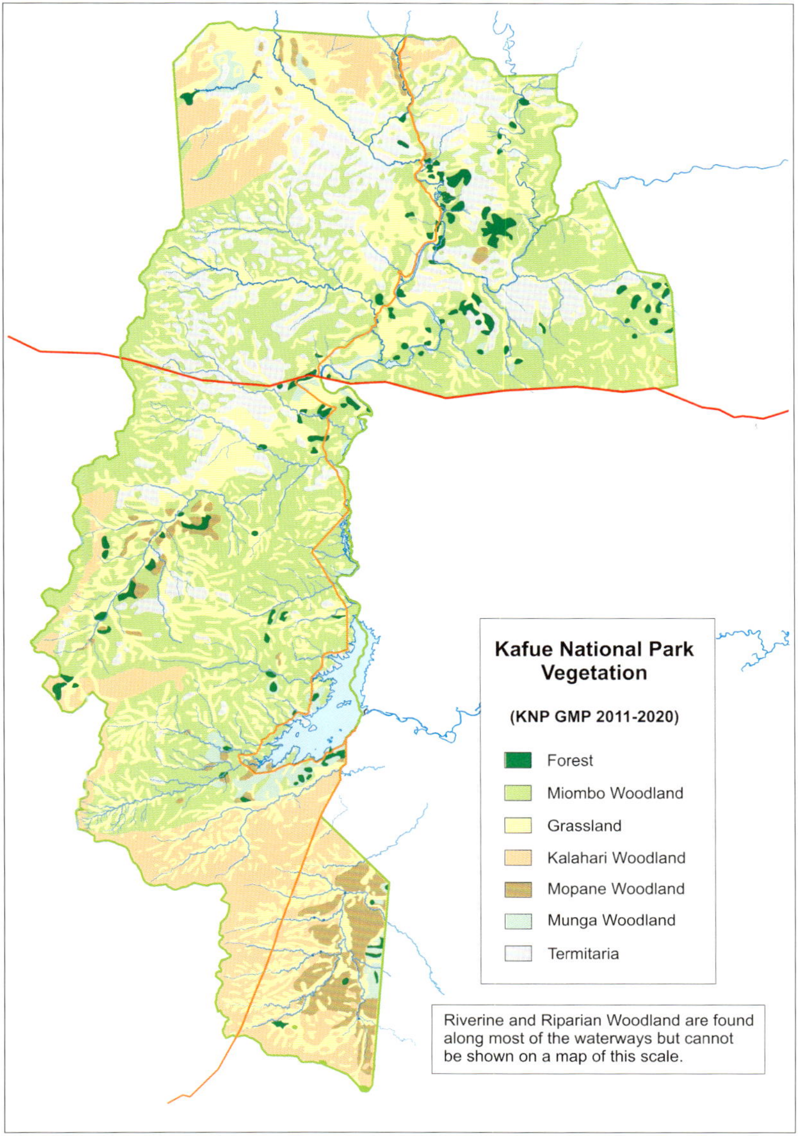
Kafue National Park
Vegetation
(KNP GMP 2011-2020)
Forest
Miombo Woodland
Grassland
Kalahari Woodland
Mopane Woodland
Munga Woodland
Termitaria
Riverine and Riparian Woodland are found along most of the waterways but cannot be shown on a map of this scale.

VEGETATION TYPES

One of the joys of visiting the KNP throughout the changing seasons (unfortunately not possible in all areas as we shall see later) is to experience the contrast from the cool conditions and low humidity of the dry season (May to October), to the wet, hot, humid conditions of the rains (November to April). It is marked by dramatic changes in plant communities and the distribution of animals, the so-called "wet season dispersal", when animals disappear from places where they are habitually seen in the dry season leaving an impression of general scarcity. The season of flowering, rapid growth and the spring flush of vegetation lasts from December to April, and is followed by several months when leaves and fruits fall, grasses turn brown and collapse and bush fires sweep through the woodlands and grasslands, leaving a trail of ash, blackened tree trunks and in some places, deceptive green clumps of short grass. Whatever time of the year you come, you will find that the following eight main vegetation types that occur in the KNP are relatively easy to recognise.

Middle Nanzhila River entering the floodplain.

1. FLOODPLAIN, DAMBO, AND RIVERINE GRASSLANDS

The grasslands of Africa once used to cover nearly 50% of the continent's surface, but a change in climate, around three million years ago, allowed trees to encroach into these grasslands and create the savannas as we know them today. KNP has some superb examples of grasslands (with over 235 species of grasses and sedges), areas noted for their high productivity and abundance of grazing animals. Good examples of floodplain grasslands are the Busanga and Nanzhila Plains, large, seasonally flooded grasslands with scattered islands of palms and fig trees. The other grassland easy to recognise and of considerable ecological significance is the drainage line grasslands of the miombo woodland named "dambos". These act as sponges for the surrounding countryside and often remain moist throughout the dry season. When burnt early in the dry season, dambos produce a green flush of new grass, invariably attracting animals such as hartebeest, roan, sable, waterbuck, zebra, reedbuck, wildebeest and oribi.

Above: The grasslands of KNP are noted for their high productivity and abundance of grazing animals.

Below: Miombo woodland covers almost half of the KNP and dominates the western boundary.

Concentrations of these species will be found on the dambo early burns almost anywhere in the Park and needless to say, this attracts poachers as well. Last but not least are the patches of riverine grassland, as the name implies adjacent to rivers and often cropped short by hippos to form attractive looking "hippo lawns".

2. MIOMBO WOODLAND

About half of the KNP is covered in miombo woodland interspersed with characteristic dambos. These extensive areas are burnt nearly every year and are dominated by *Brachystegia* and *Julbernardia* trees. With the exception of the dambos, miombo woodland gives the superficial appearance of being almost devoid of wildlife and of little interest to the visitor. Slow down and look out

for important bird species (see the important localities in Chapter 3) and try to visit towards the end of the dry season to experience an astonishing array of the spring colours of red, pink and yellow that emerge in the wonderful spectacle of the flush of leaves in the miombo canopy. The red pigments (anthocyanins) responsible for this are an ecological adaptation that may protect the leaves from ultra-violet rays of bright sunlight, and provide a manifestation equal if not superior to the heralded "fall" of the northern hemisphere.

3. TERMITARIA TYPES

Large, often vegetated, termite mounds (termitaria) are seen throughout KNP, and are prominent in both miombo and mopane. Individual termite mounds may be formed over as much as 700 years by various species of the fungus-growing termites, and be 9 m high and 20–30 m in diameter at the base. What is particularly interesting is that the soils in the termitaria have more mineral nitrogen and available phosphorus than the soils of the surrounding areas, making them what ecologists refer to as "nutrient hotspots" in the otherwise nutrient-poor miombo woodland. Not surprisingly, the termitaria are usually well browsed and their grasses and herbs, particularly where trees are absent or scarce, are frequently cropped short. These mounds then form fire-free islands and continue to provide browse and grazing throughout the long winter months (dry season) when fires have removed almost all the surrounding vegetation.

Typical termitaria vegetation that is common in many parts of the Park especially the south where these nutrient-rich islands usually survive bush fires and thus provide cover and food for animals throughout the year.

4. FOREST AND THICKET

There are a few places where dry, deciduous forests and thickets are found that are free from annual burning. The term "forest" in this context refers to the Zambezi teak or *Baikiaea plurijuga* forest on well-drained Zambezi sands. The Ngoma Forest best represents these and there are a few patches on the western boundary at the source of the Luansanda. Thicket, known locally as *"Mutemwa"*, is often the understorey of *Baikiaea* forests. It is commonly an early stage in the re-establishment of forest in abandoned village garden sites, and it sometimes occurs in areas heavily degraded by late season fires. The thicket north of Ngoma is a fine example, where you may be fortunate to see the highly venomous gaboon viper or the giant stick insect, which grows to over 400 mm or more.

Above: Ngoma Forest in the autumn with a tall teak tree surrounded by a strangler fig.

5. MOPANE WOODLAND

This type of woodland is easily recognised by its open, park-like appearance and by few tree species other than the tree from which it gets its name, *Colophospermum mopane*. There are large areas in the south-east, between Dundumwezi and Kalenje and along the Musa and Mungosiya Rivers. Elsewhere, mopane is found in thin, isolated patches, the most interesting being very close to Treetops Camp, where there is a small patch that is separated by over 100 km from the nearest stand of mopane adjacent to the Hook Bridge on the eastern bank of the Kafue.

Below: Mopane woodland is typically found growing on shallow alkaline soils, often alluvial (deposited by a river) and not well drained.

You are likely to see many more mammals in the mopane woodlands than in miombo. Look out for impala, warthog, kudu, reedbuck, zebra, roan,

Top: Acacia and monkey bread savanna on clay soil north of Chunga.

Below: Suffrutex savanna characterised by low growing woody perennials.

eland, buffalo and elephant for a start, and notice the places where elephants have knocked down mature mopane trees and then heavily browsed the regrowth, in so doing providing browse for the smaller species at a lower level. This aspect of elephant feeding behaviour is too frequently overlooked by those who judge the pushing over and breaking of trees by elephants as simply damage to vegetation.

6. SAVANNA

A savanna (sometimes spelt "savannah"), is easily recognised as a grassy woodland with a significant woody plant component, but where the trees are sufficiently small or widely spaced so that the canopy does not close. The two most widespread savanna types in the KNP are the monkeybread *(Piliostigma thoningii)* plains on clay soils between Chunga and Kafwala, and the suffrutex savanna (characterised by low-growing woody perennials) on the dry to semi-moist edges of badly degraded miombo or *Baikiaea* woodland near Ngoma, in the old village areas of Katinti north of the Musa River and on the edge of the Busanga Plain. Suffrutex savanna has come into being as a consequence of too-frequent fires, but these areas are often good for wildlife, particularly to the south west of Nkala loop near Ngoma, where wildebeest, oribi, zebra, waterbuck, sable, reedbuck and roan are often seen feeding, especially if there is a green flush after early burning.

7. SWAMP

There is only one true swamp in the Park and that is the papyrus *Cyperus papyrus* swamp at the northern end of the Busanga Plain. At present this can only be visited on foot or by canoes, but worth the effort as it is the main place in KNP where sitatunga occur, often in close proximity to crocodiles, hippos and herds of red lechwe.

8. RIVERINE OR RIPARIAN WOODLAND

Arguably the most important scenic and recreational features of the Park are the unpolluted rivers and streams and, most appealingly perhaps, the nature of the Kafue River itself - long stretches of smooth deep water, pools, rapids, palm-covered islands, grass-covered banks, and an almost continuous strip of shady evergreen gallery riparian woodland, with some *Phoenix, Borassus* and *Hyphaene* palms. It is worth slowing down and spending time in these scenically attractive areas, where over 150 species of birds have been recorded.

Top: Canoes enable visitors to access the swamps of the Busanga Plain.

Below: The Kafue River has extensive areas of attractive riverine woodland.

WILDLIFE OF THE KNP

The Park has many attractions, but even for those who come just to relax in unspoilt wilderness, or to go fishing along the banks of the incomparable Kafue River, nearly every visitor will want to see and experience the larger mammals of

Most of the breeding population of the Zambian endemic black-cheeked lovebird is found in the south of the KNP, with the Nanzhila area being a prime site.

the KNP, and an increasing number are enthusiastic birders. For first-time visitors to Africa, it is so important to appreciate that the best wildlife experiences will nearly always be early mornings (often not too popular with northern hemisphere visitors) and late afternoons. If you are being guided, you will soon learn where to look and what to look out for, but if you are on your own, *drive slowly* and look out for vultures, newly broken vegetation, fresh tracks and fresh droppings, all good indicators of the presence of larger mammals and a hopeful sign that predators will also be in the vicinity.

According to the 2010 IUCN Red List of Threatened Species, Zambia has six mammal species that are rated as "Vulnerable", two "Endangered" and one "Critically Endangered", of which elephant, lion, cheetah and hippopotamus are rated as Vulnerable, wild dog is Endangered, and black rhino Critically Endangered. The Kafue mole-rat is listed as a Vulnerable species, and although it has only been recorded from the Kafue Flats, it could be found in the Park. Black rhino have not been sighted since the early 1990s and regrettably almost certainly no longer occur in KNP.

There are 12 Vulnerable and one Endangered bird species listed for Zambia, of which the black-cheeked lovebird, shoebill, grey crowned crane, slaty egret, lesser kestrel, wattled crane, Chaplin's barbet, lappet faced vulture and white headed vulture are Vulnerable species recorded in the KNP. There are six Vulnerable, two Endangered and two Critically Endangered species of fish recorded from Zambia, of which the three-spot tilapia and greenhead tilapia are Vulnerable species recorded for the KNP.

MAMMALS

Kafue stands out as the Park where more antelope species have been recorded than in any other park anywhere. In addition some species, such as roan and sable, that you will find easily in KNP, are rated as rare in Kruger National Park, with which Kafue is often compared. This unique array reflects the diversity of the ecosystems and the range of habitats that the Park contains. The shapes of antelope, their colour, feeding habits and behaviour show how they have adapted to local conditions by natural selection and gradual evolution. Always accompanying them are all the other large and small mammals that form the web of predator and prey, which never fails to provide interest and excitement and often great risk for those who protect them and for people who do not take care when they confront them.

Although Kafue protects at least 160 species of mammals, a question that is often raised is why the Park has no giraffe, rhino or tsessebe? Up until the 1980's KNP had black rhinos throughout, and for a while after the Park was formed, their numbers and distribution were growing. Sadly, all were killed in the orgy of rhino poaching that swept through Africa in the 1970s and 1980s. For giraffe and tsessebe, their stories are very different. It is said that giraffe were never here, but of course that depends upon how far back the records go and with two isolated populations, one in western Zambia and another in the Luangwa Valley and the fact that they are doing well on far-flung private land in similar habitats elsewhere in Zambia, it is interesting to speculate what quirks of climate, flooding, fire or indeed the hand of man, caused their absence. In the case of tsessebe, there are two areas of well-separated open floodplain grassland in Zambia where they do occur, one near Lake Bangweulu and the other mainly on the west bank of the Zambezi near the habitat of giraffe. In between the Kafue floodplains and the Busanga Plain seem to provide abundant suitable habitat, but there are no tsessebe. It could be that their narrow habitat of open grassland on the edges of floodplains may make then exceptionally vulnerable to fire or excessive hunting.

The following short descriptions of the larger mammals present in the Park will help you with their identification. Although there is of course no guarantee that you will see all of them even if you stay for a month at a time, your visit will no doubt be enhanced by using the "spotting lists" in Chapter 6.

ANTELOPE SPECIES RECORDED IN KNP

Blue duiker
Bushbuck
Common duiker
Eland
Grysbok
Hartebeest
Impala
Klipspringer
Kudu
Oribi
Puku
Red lechwe
Reedbuck
Roan antelope
Sable antelope
Sitatunga
Steenbok
Waterbuck (Defassa)
Waterbuck (Common)
Wildebeest
Yellow-backed duiker

Recently one visitor to the KNP recorded no less than 33 species of the larger mammals in just three days on and around the Nanzhila Plains alone; a wonderful illustration of the great potential of this Park for observing and recording its superb diversity.

Elephant: Elephants can be seen throughout the Park, an important species on account of their size and the impact that they have on the environment, opening up woodland, knocking down trees and making pathways for smaller animals to reach river banks, lagoons and pans. KNP has a healthy population of about 5,000 that ranges throughout the Park and the Game Management Areas and very often beyond, possibly even across national boundaries to countries within the vast Kavango-Zambezi Transfrontier Conservation Area (see Chapter 4).

Hippopotamus: Generally confined to the principal rivers in the KNP and at the mouths of other larger tributaries of the Kafue. They occasionally wander further upstream to Ngoma on the Nkala and to Nangandwe Pool at Nanzhila Plains Safari Camp on the Kasha River, main tributary of the Nanzhila. Along the main Kafue River they are well spread out but in the dry season there are places on the Busanga Plain and along the Lufupa River where they become packed together in large numbers. They are rarely seen far from water during the day, coming out to graze at night, giving rise to the characteristic "hippo lawns" of short grass.

Buffalo: Although the total number of buffalo in the KNP has decreased, there appears to be a good recovery in some places in the last few years and today they can be found throughout the Park, with herds of 400–500 being seen regularly in the Busanga, Chunga and Lake Itezhi-Tezhi areas. They have always been the preferred prey of lion, and the increasing sightings of lion suggest that buffalo are holding their own in areas where there is adequate protection and more tourism. Look out for them on the open grasslands, dambos, woodland edges and thickets. Both sexes have horns, which are much more heavily bossed in the males.

Burchell's zebra: Zebra are to be seen on most routes, but the best places for them are around the Busanga Plain, near Chunga and Mukambi, in the north-east and in the Ngoma-Dundumwezi open grassland and floodplain habitats. Unfortunately, like wildebeest, they have been over-hunted for their skins and tails, which fetch good prices in illegal markets. Happily, now there are several well-established breeding herds which indicates that they are doing well in most places. Look out for foals in the period from July to September and listen for the characteristic zebra contact call, especially at night.

Eland: The world's largest member of the Tragelaphini, spiral-horned antelope, growing up to a height of 178 cm (70 inches), that at one time was common throughout the Park in sizeable herds. Eland numbers and distribution are affected by selective illegal hunting because of the quantity and good quality of its meat, for its hide, and for its tail, which is used in the handicraft industry as a fly whisk. The eland is a selective browser-grazer that has a large home range where it is a nomadic wanderer, often covering long distances to seek food, mainly on shrubs and early flushes of grasses. Both sexes have horns.

Kudu: This is another large spiral-horned antelope and, unlike the eland, the female does not have horns. Kudu are mainly browsers and, although the species is widely distributed, they are usually seen on the edges of dense woodland near watercourses and in thickets. They are commonly seen in the south of the Park feeding on the large termitaria in the Nanzhila Plains and in nearby mopane woodland. It is a resilient species and appears to be recovering in all the places where it is being well protected.

Sable antelope: Sable is another spectacular species that is much sought-after by antelope enthusiasts. Mature adult males change colour from tawny brown to almost jet-black, often seen leading large herds of females with their young that are produced in July-September period. The species is well-represented throughout most of the woodland/grassland habitats staying more within the tree line than roan. Sightings in the Park are common in the north-east, and along the Nkala and Shakalongo Plain in the south. Both sexes have horns but they are shorter and more slender in the female.

Roan antelope: This large animal lives in herds that are led by one male and which have well-established home ranges. Roan belongs to the group that frequents woodland/savannas/grasslands, never too far from water. The species is distributed throughout the Park in herds of 30 or more that are being commonly seen these days in the Nanzhila and around the Nkala – Kaunga track in the south, usually found feeding on the miombo woodland and dambo edges. There are highly visible resident herds on the Busanga Plain. Both sexes have horns.

Blue wildebeest: Restricted to the west side (the right bank) of the Kafue River, with herds of 20-30 along the Nanzhila in the south, the Nkala drainage, in the Chunga area and in the north from old Moshi up the Lufupa River and on the Busanga Plain towards the northern boundary. For reasons unknown the species is very unevenly distributed even in suitable habitat (open miombo woodland and woodland/grassland edges) throughout their range. Calving peaks during the vulnerable period of August - September. They are often targeted by poachers for their tails, that are used as fly whisks and status symbols. Both sexes have horns which are more heavily bossed in the males.

Lichtenstein's hartebeest: In contrast with sable and roan, this species is distinguished by its uniform red/brown colour with relatively short and sharply twisted lyre-shaped horns, which are present in both sexes. Hartebeest prefer miombo woodland, and they occur throughout the Park, usually in smaller herds than roan or sable. Like sable, the calving period is in the late dry season, at which time unfortunately most of their habitat has been burnt. Hunters know that the green flush of grass that often follows these burns attracts hartebeest, and it is in these burnt areas that you are most likely to find herds grazing with their young in July-September.

Waterbuck: You will notice from the antelope list that two waterbuck are mentioned. *Kobus ellipsiprymnus defassa* has a large white patch on its rump and has always been one of the most commonly seen waterbuck throughout the Park, whereas *Kobus ellipsiprymnus ellipsiprymnus,* which has a slim white crescent around its rump, was not supposed to be found in the Park until 12 May 1968, when a solitary female was observed near Ngoma. This intrepid wanderer led to a hybrid population on the Nkala River that seems to have disappeared, an aberration the simple consequences of erratic behaviour on the part of a single individual. Any new sightings would be received with great interest! Horns only in males.

Reedbuck: Reedbuck, like the red lechwe, is another species that is recovering well after years of excessive pressure. This is a medium-sized dull brown/grey animal that is lightly built with slender legs and horns that initially curve backwards and then arch widely apart and forwards, but only in males. They always live near water, preferably where there are reeds or other low cover, staying either solitarily or in small family groups in small home ranges. Their restricted habitat, slim build, and habit of leaping away with tail raised and shrill whistle repeated when alarmed, makes identification relatively easy.

Impala: The gazelle-like impala is noted for its spectacular jumping when disturbed. Jousting between males during the rutting season at the end of the rains is also worth watching. The species is well-distributed throughout the Park favouring shady woodland-grassland edges where they mainly graze during the rains, changing to more browsing during the dry season. They have small home ranges and are always found at established locations, Chunga being one where the large resident population is easy for you to find at almost any time. Horns only in males.

Puku: This is a species that is recovering well in suitable habitat throughout the Park, especially around Lake Itezhi-Tezhi, near Mukambi Lodge and along the Kafue River up to the Busanga Plain. Its remarkable absence in the Nanzhila area is often mentioned since there is no good reason why it does not occur there, other than its susceptibility to over hunting, and it is thus likely to have disappeared from there in recent times. It is a grazer living and grazing on floodplains and along the woodland edge near rivers and streams. Horns only in males.

Oribi: Another small antelope that is usually easy to identify by its reddish-brown coat, short straight horns and the fact that it is nearly always found grazing solitarily or in pairs in open grassland. It has an upright stance and an unusual way of running jerkily, known as "pronking", with a characteristic action of leaping in the air with arched back and all legs held stiffly in the air. Oribi make a loud shrill whistle when disturbed and, since it seldom leaves open grassland, even when chased, it is easily hunted and therefore exceptionally vulnerable to poaching. Horns only in males.

Red lechwe: The only secure population of this sub-species of lechwe in the whole country is found on the Busanga area in the far north on KNP, where you will find them grazing in the open floodplains in large herds. Lechwe will quickly bound off into water to avoid terrestrial predators, since they are relatively slow movers on land but are exceptionally quick and powerful in water. Zambia also has secure populations of the Kafue lechwe and black lechwe, the two other subspecies. Horns only in males.

Bushbuck: One of the most attractive of the smaller antelope, noted for its highly variable colouration of light to very dark brown, with clear, narrow, white stripes and spots. The males are appreciably larger than the females, and become darker with age. They have short, almost straight horns that have one or two spirals. Bushbuck prefer thickets and fringes of woodland where there is dense cover, very often along rivers and streams. Although usually shy and elusive, they are frequently seen standing beside tracks that pass close to the Kafue River, such as Riverside Drive north of Lufupa River Camp, particularly early in the morning and late afternoon/evening. Horns only in males.

Sitatunga: The ultra-shy spiral-horned sitatunga is restricted in KNP to the far north in the middle of the Busanga Plain. It has solitary habits with very small home ranges within a habitat that is restricted to papyrus swamps and reed-beds, where they can be seen grazing on tiny patches of short-cropped grass at dawn just as the mist rises from the swamp or late in the afternoon. The sitatunga is well-adapted to its semi-aquatic way of life with the longest hoofs of any antelope which splay out, enabling it to walk on mud and floating beds of vegetation. Horns only in males.

Common duiker: A small and highly adaptable, yet at times surprisingly elusive, territorial antelope that can survive close to human habitation and in degraded woodland, preferring miombo where there is some undergrowth and ground cover. Some authorities refer to it as *"the most successful bovid species in Africa"*. It is widespread throughout Africa and the KNP, even in woodlands that have been badly burnt. It will drink water when available but can survive for long periods without. "Duiker" is Afrikaans for "diver", a name derived from its habit of plunging into and concealing itself in thick vegetation. Horns only in males.

Blue duiker: This small, dark antelope is very shy and secretive, and as a consequence is rarely seen, with observations made even more difficult as the elusive species has a restricted habitat confined to forests and thickets. It is occasionally sighted in the Ngoma Forest, in the thickets north of Ngoma and in the north-east in the Hippo Lodge and Mushingashi dense woodland and thicket habitats. With indigenous forests shrinking rapidly throughout most of Africa, blue duiker sightings anywhere are likely to become more difficult. Both sexes have horns.

Yellow-backed duiker: Limited to the dense woodland to the north-west in the Kasolo-Kampinga and Park boundary areas and to similar habitat in the north-east. Although the yellow-backed duiker is the largest of all the 15 duiker species found in Africa (weighing up to 70 kg) it is rarely seen in the KNP, but is easily recognizable with its short and glossy coat that is dark brown to black in colour, with the exception of a patch of yellow hairs on their rumps (hence the name). It is usually nocturnal, spending most of the day resting in beds (called forms) from under tree trunks to the top of termite mounds. Both sexes have horns.

Grysbok: One of the smallest antelope that can be distinguished from all the others not only on account of its size, standing less than 55 cm high, but also its grizzled dark reddish-brown colour with clear white flecks. With this cryptic colouration and secretive nature, it is easily overlooked. Its rounded rump which, is higher than the shoulder, gives it a compact hunched appearance that helps identification. Grysbok are solitary and are found in miombo woodland where there is some undergrowth, such as the woodland on the northern edge of the teak forest near Ngoma. Horns only in males.

Klipspringer: Similar in height to the steenbok but with a much heavier and more compact build, distinguishing features include a goat-like shape with a compact head and rounded ears and an unusual stance and gait of standing and walking on the blunt tips of its hooves, hopping sometimes in short leaps from rock to rock. The species is seldom seen these days in KNP and is totally confined to rocky hillside habitats, where the only records are the extensive Shibatwa Hills west of the Spinal Road above Lake Itezhi-Tezhi and the low hills near Dundumwezi Entrance Gate in the south. Horns only in males.

Steenbok: A small antelope of the woodland edge, confined to the drier miombo in the southern part of the Park, from the Musa River catchment towards Mulobezi, even in places where water is very scarce, but seldom on hillsides. Distinguished from the common duiker by a more slender body and neck with longer legs, a more upright stance and prominently long and broad ears and a very short tail. It may be seen standing in open woodland where it defends its territory, but as soon as it has seen you it takes fright and darts swiftly away into cover, often lying down after it has covered a short distance. Horns only in males.

Warthog: This is one of the commonest large mammals (and arguably the ugliest!) that can be found everywhere, generally running along with its tufted tail stuck up vertically or feeding in small family groups. It utilises a wide range of habitats and is frequently seen near permanent pools in clay soils where it is able to "puddle" and roll in wet mud. Despite being a favourite prey for lion, leopard and cheetah, it is doing well throughout the park. Warthog will often graze in and around camp sites, and soon become habituated, but be warned – they are formidable fighters if cornered and can be dangerous.

Bushpig: The frequent sightings of these large wild pigs are an encouraging recent development, because despite their mainly nocturnal habits, they are being seen all over KNP and often during daylight hours. They prefer forests and riverine vegetation, feeding on roots, tubers, grass and almost any carrion or fallen fruit in a clumsy and disruptive way, often leaving a chaotic wake of upturned soil. The bushpig lies up in dense cover, but when it is encountered moving from one feeding area to another, it is easily identified and distinguished from warthog by its bulky shape and long line of thick white hairs that stick up along its back.

Lion: KNP has built up a deserved reputation for its large prides of lion and it may be the source of another success story as numbers appear to be on the increase throughout the Park, a reflection of the general increase in the numbers of prey on which lion depend. Buffalo and hartebeest appear to be their preferred prey so keep a look out for them whenever you see these species. On the Busanga Plain it is not unusual to easily see two or three prides on a single drive and they are also relatively common on the Shishamba Loop and around Lake Itezhi-Tezhi.

Leopard: Although leopard in KNP are also on the increase despite so much persecution for their skins, they are much more difficult to find than lion because they are mainly nocturnal, secretive and extremely well camouflaged. They are most often seen where there are plenty of impala, puku and reedbuck on which they like to feed within territories that cover 50-60 km². They are known for being agile and skilful silent hunters and for taking their kills up trees to keep them away from hyaena and jackal. Night drives are the most rewarding time to see leopard, with the Lufupa area in particular having the best reputation for sightings.

Cheetah: This is one of Africa's charismatic species, the fastest mammalian predator capable of reaching speeds of up to 100 km/hr over a short distance. Cheetah sightings in KNP have also increased recently and after being a species that was "seldom seen" it is now observed frequently in parts of the Park where the smaller antelope have become abundant. It is generally considered a species favouring "open country" but it is increasingly being seen in the Park close to thickets and in open woodland on the edges of dambos.

Wild dog: Although the wild dog is regarded as one of Africa's most threatened species today, it is still relatively widespread throughout KNP, which is now rated as one of Africa's "most important refuges for wild dog and cheetah", with at least 35 known localities where packs are to be found. Regarded as one of the world's most efficient mammalian predators, its recent decline can be attributed to diseases (rabies and distemper) passed on by contacts with domestic dogs, and lion predation on both adults and wild dog puppies. They are also ruthlessly persecuted by farmers if they start marauding into livestock farming land.

Spotted hyaena: For many years thought to be just a voracious scavenger, the spotted hyaena is now recognised as an efficient and powerful predator in its own right. It has exceptionally powerful jaws for tearing away meat and chewing bones, leaving droppings that become white as soon as they dry out. The species is well represented and is frequently sighted. It is easy to recognise with a head that appears to thrust forward on a thick neck above very strong shoulders and with downward sloping hindquarters and a shaggy dark brown/grey roughly spotted coat. The wild laughing and screaming sounds that it makes at night can be quite frightening and will never be forgotten.

Side-striped jackal: The name for this species of jackal comes from the clear white stripe along its side, sometimes edged with some black, which is quite distinct from the black-backed jackal that has a prominent black patch spreading from head to tail and is not found in Zambia. It is omnivorous and a part-time nocturnal predator making the well-known jackal's yelping howls or distant plaintive cry. It is often seen scavenging on remnants of kills made by larger predators or when feeding on smaller mammals, mainly rats and mice and even insects.

Porcupine: This is an unmistakable nocturnal animal that you will come across on night drives almost anywhere, but especially along bush tracks in areas such as the Nanzhila and towards the west where sandy soils predominate. Porcupines shelter and breed in disused aardvark burrows. They are exclusively vegetarian and have few predators other than lion, which often come off badly in encounters when porcupine quills become embedded in their paws, sometimes making them so lame that they cannot hunt effectively. Notorious as crop-raiders, the extension of agricultural land throughout Zambia has probably benefitted the spread of the species outside of National Parks.

Springhare: This is another fascinating nocturnal animal, which bears a remarkable resemblance to a mini-kangaroo in that its hind legs are far longer than the front, enabling it to hop long distances in each step. Little is known about their distribution in the park except that they are easy to see in sandy soil areas especially in the south near Nanzhila. Although adults weigh less than 3 kg, it is of significant economic importance, especially in neighbouring Botswana where it is the most important wild animal in the human diet, and a valuable source of skins for domestic use.

Rock dassie (hyrax): Surprisingly, the closest living relatives of this small mammal, which weighs between 3-4 kg are the elephants and the marine dugongs, with which the dassie shares several similar anatomical features. The fossil record shows that all three species are descended from a common ancestor some 40 million years ago. The rock dassie lives on rock outcrops with crevices for overnight shelter, browsing and grazing during the day, and leaving their droppings in the same place in small mounds so that when it rains these concentrated organic pellets are washed down the rocks to boost the flush of spring vegetation below with nutrients which otherwise would be lacking.

Pangolin: The pangolin is unlike any other African mammal, being covered in plate-like scales that afford it protection against predators. When threatened, it is able to roll up quickly into a ball to protect its soft face and belly and is easily overlooked or mistaken for a small rock. It feeds on ants and termites, which it sniffs out from beneath the soil surface, inserting its 25 cm long saliva-covered tongue into the ground and withdrawing it covered with the insects that it quickly swallows whole as it has no teeth. It is usually nocturnal and generally solitary so that it is only seen infrequently and mostly in habitats where termite mounds are abundant well away from laterite or stony ground.

THE LESSER MAMMALS

Servals favour open grasslands where they hunt for rats and mice.

All too often the desire to see the bigger mammals means that the large number of fascinating smaller and mainly nocturnal species, which require much more patience and careful exploration, are overlooked. The mammals list at the end of the book shows just how many there are in the Park. Many of these are best seen during night drives. They include the serval, genets, civets, ratel or honey badger, and the two diminutive and nocturnal primates (thick-tailed bushbaby and night ape). Mongooses are another group of small, mainly nocturnal predators that have long slender bodies and sharp teeth but differ from the genets by having general dull grey/brown coats with the exception of the banded mongoose that has clear black stripes across its whole body making it easy to identify. There are eight species in KNP, of which the white-tailed mongoose with its obvious long bushy white tail and paler overall grey colour with dark legs

The honey badger is an avid digger looking for rodents, scorpions and beetles.

The white-tailed mongoose is the largest mongoose of the eight species found in the KNP.

is easy to identify. The slender mongoose is much smaller and is probably the most frequently seen, crossing rapidly on the road or stalking its prey in roadside bushes.

For those who are prepared to spend time sitting by the waterways, look out for spotted-necked otters and clawless otters. Little is known about their overall distribution but although they have been heavily persecuted for their skins in the past, they are now recovering well and are often seen, especially along the middle Kafue River. If you are very lucky, you might encounter an aardvark (or antbear), a shy and rare animal, but strictly nocturnal. Your best chances are in the central and southern areas where there are active termite mounds and grass/woodland edge habitats.

Thick-tailed bushbabies forage at night for insects and fruit.

The aardvark digs into the ground for ants and termites, but this 50 – 60 kg animal is rarely seen as it only starts foraging late at night.

BIRDS

KNP is rated as one of Zambia's "Important Bird Areas" with 494 species recorded within its borders and a further 22 species that have been found in the adjacent Game Management Areas. Just as for the mammals, the number of species is a reflection of the diversity of habitats. Unfortunately, as for all wildlife, annual uncontrolled bush fires have a serious effect on the distribution and numbers and only when this destructive phenomenon declines or disappears altogether will natural abundance come about. Nevertheless birding is nearly always productive, especially during the rains when there is plenty of food and cover; this is also the nesting time for many species. The Park has several Zambezian endemics and near-endemics, which are there to be found and observed, but nowhere as easily as the mammals described earlier. Prominent among these are the black-cheeked lovebird, Chaplin's barbet, racket-tailed roller, pale-billed hornbill, miombo pied barbet, Fulleborn's longclaw, central bearded scrub-robin, red-capped crombec, Böhm's flycatcher and Sousa's shrike.

The bright orange-red legs of the furtive African finfoot are conspicuous in flight.

African skimmers feed when in flight by trailing their lower mandibles in water "skimming" for fish.

Juvenile Pel's fishing-owl with characteristic adult plumage on its back.

Black-backed barbet.

For good sightings of species with a much wider distribution in Africa, but not seen that regularly, the riverine habitats as well as the large seasonal dambos and pools are good viewing areas for species such as the white-backed night heron, African finfoot, rock pratincole, African skimmer, Lady Ross's turaco, Pel's fishing-owl, half-collared kingfisher and black-backed barbet. In the riparian thickets Böhm's bee-eater and giant kingfisher are common and in the thickets north of Ngoma and the under-storey of the Ngoma Teak Forest, crested guineafowl are the speciality.

Crested guineafowl.

More details of where to go to find the species of interest to you are given in Chapter 3 and can be accessed easily through the index.

REPTILES

Very little is known about the reptiles in the Park, apart from the occurrence of 44 species of snakes, widespread distribution of crocodiles, terrapins found along streams and in seasonal pools, tortoises, of which the attractively marked leopard tortoise is the most commonly seen, and monitor lizards (see the checklist in Chapter 6).

The Nile monitor is one of Africa's largest reptiles and found along all Kafue's waterways, where it is frequently seen hunting and scavenging for small animals of all kinds, fish, frogs, snakes, crocodile eggs and carrion.

The highly coloured but rarely sighted, slow moving and seriously poisonous Gaboon viper and the relatively harmless savanna monitor are two species of note: the Gaboon viper is found in the thickets north of Ngoma, which is the southern limit of its geographical range in the Park, stretching southwards from the tropical forests of West Africa. The savanna monitor that is known to inhabit the sandstone and granite hills to the north and west of Lake Itezhi-Tezhi is rarely seen, but this could change once the Spinal Road is fully opened up to the north of the lake.

Crocodiles are found in all the major tributaries of the Kafue. Other areas where they are most numerous are the middle and upper Lufupa River, including the channels on the Busanga Plain and Lake Itezhi-Tezhi. Generally, the crocodile population is now recovering successfully after being greatly reduced by legal and illegal hunting, especially on the middle stretches of the Kafue River.

Above: The Gaboon viper is one of the most colourful and deadliest of snakes but it is not seen often as its habitat is dense woodland and forest. KNP is the southernmost part of its range in Zambia.

Below: The Nile crocodile grows up to nearly 5 metres in length and although it spends most of its time lurking in the water it is often seen sunning itself on rocks and sandbanks along all the waterways in the Park. It is an immensely powerful predator and will attack almost any animal as well as humans when it is hungry.

Reed frogs add a superb dimension to KNP's extraordinary celebration of colour and diversity.

AMPHIBIANS

Amphibians have not been systematically studied in the Park even though all the genera and over 50% of the species known to occur in Zambia are probably represented here. Our checklist of amphibians includes ones that are either known to occur or likely to occur. This list was provided by Don Broadley and it should be used as a basis for doing research on this fascinating group of animals, some of which, such as tiny reed frogs, have exquisite shapes and colours.

(Don Broadley's 1971 book, entitled *The Reptiles and Amphibians of Zambia,* is still the only definitive publication on these two classes of animals, providing identification keys, ecological notes and distribution records).

FISH

The fishes of the Park have not been properly surveyed and little is known, other than in broad generalizations, on the occurrence, distribution and ecology of species. There is some information in ZAWA records about the fishes of the Park and about the activities of the village fishermen who have rights to seasonally fish in the Busanga area, the middle Kafue River and Nanzhila areas, and these do give an indication of the existence of certain species and in some cases, how likely they are to be caught. For the sport angler fishing is good and can be done in many places. Permits are obtainable from ZAWA or at lodges and camps. More details on what to catch and where are given in Chapter 3.

Hamerkops can be seen throughout KNP feeding on the Park's abundant fish resources.

But fish are much more than just an attraction for anglers, and are worth looking

Killifish are found only in seasonal pools and even ditches that become totally dry and this is where they complete their remarkable life cycle each year.

out for at certain times of the year, even on land! For example, the climbing fish (*Ctenopoma multispinis*) can be seen in the early rains propelling itself out of the water in large numbers across wet grass, using its serrated pectoral fins to spring in short leaps, moving across the ground en masse from one pool to another. Among the other remarkable adaptations to seasonal changes, is the life cycle of the killifish, a small, superbly colourful fish that lives in scattered seasonal pools. When the pools dry out the adult fish spawn and leave their eggs to aestivate in the mud, after which the adults die. During the first rains in the following season and as the pools fill up, the eggs hatch, the fish grow and the cycle is repeated. Added to these unusual habits is the ability of the black barbel (catfish) to similarly bury themselves in drying mud at the bottom and sides of clay-lined pools to aestivate during the late dry season and reappear again in the succeeding rains, their movements attracting marabou storks and other predators.

INVERTEBRATES

There is very little known scientifically about the invertebrate fauna in the Park but it is an immense and important field on which rewarding studies could be undertaken particularly on Tsetse (*Glossina* spp.), which have been responsible for substantial modification to Park development in the past and probably in the future. Bilharzia snails (Mollusca) are also of economic importance as vectors of bilharzia or schistosomiasis in man so that planned tourism development, especially on Lake Itezhi-Tezhi

Termite mound in miombo woodland.

needs to take the presence of bilharzia snails into consideration. Terrestrial micro-fauna and its relation to fire is of prime ecological importance, especially termites, which are recognised as by far the most important invertebrates in tropical ecosystems where they play a wholly beneficial role in plant diversity, and the development of Termitaria vegetation types described earlier.

Of great importance and one so often overlooked in the role of National Parks is the conservation of pollinator species. Pollination is arguably one of the mechanisms most critical to the maintenance of life on earth. So many of today's agriculturists are calling attention to the declining diversity of bees, butterflies and other insects. Pollinator services associated with agricultural ecosystems are essential for global food security, with up to three-quarters of the world's crops relying on insects and other animals to carry pollen from one plant to the next. It should be self-evident that the decline or loss of these carriers will inevitably exacerbate the frequency and scale of food riots. Thus a place like KNP is of enormous economic importance as a source for the region's pollinators. For invertebrates there are many threats that they face everywhere mainly due to disturbances caused by burning, land clearing, quarrying, construction, tree felling, cutting of grass and trampling of vegetation. The biggest hazard is undoubtedly the destruction of micro-habitats cause by bush fires.

CLIMATE OF THE KNP

Zambia has an outstandingly pleasant climate – there is a general pattern of warm sunny days, but

Lightning storm in the early rains - northern Kafue.

it seldom becomes unbearably hot and evenings and nights are usually cool, even in the hot season. During a year, despite occasions when it can be dull and cloudy, there is a remarkable average of about eight hours of sunshine a day. The Park lies between the higher rainfall areas to the north-west of the country and the lower rainfall areas to the south. In the north of the Park the average seasonal rainfall slightly exceeds 1,020 mm and in the south seldom exceeds 800 mm. It rains mostly between November and April, averaging 750 mm (30 inches) per season overall. Mid-day temperatures range between an average of 24°C (75°F) and 30°C (86°F), with the hottest month in October and the coldest in July. Frost occurs occasionally during the winter. Average dry

season relative humidity is 40% (often much lower than that) with cool easterly breezes that strengthen during a spell of a few weeks after the end of the rains.

The outstanding characteristic of the climate is the marked seasonality of rainfall that divides the year into a rainy season, usually of six or seven months, and a dry season. For most purposes, appreciation of this single divide is probably enough, since events relating to the growth of plants and dispersal of animals generally coincide with the length of these two periods. The bioclimatic factor that is of most significance in the abundance of animals, their ecological and physiological adaptations and their seasonal movements, is the amount, distribution and duration of rainfall.

Opposite: Storm over Lake Itezhi-Tezhi.

> *A visit to KNP surely echoes Sir Julian Huxley's words of fifty years ago when he wrote about Africa's wildlife and natural habitats: "To see large animals going about their natural business in their own natural way, assured and unafraid, is one of the most exciting and moving experiences in the world, comparable with the sight of a noble building or the hearing of a great symphony or mass. A processional frieze of antelopes moving across the African horizon rivals any theatrical spectacle. The world at large cannot afford to let this great human resource disappear."*

PLANNING YOUR TRIP

SPECIAL ATTRACTIONS OF THE KNP

The Kafue National Park presents a wide range of exceptional opportunities to appreciate wildlife and genuine unspoilt wilderness at its very best. The extraordinary diversity places the Park in a special category of its own, with the 160 species of mammals and over 500 species of birds in untransformed landscapes where there are no sights, sounds or smells of human intrusion. The KNP is unquestionably an outstanding destination for those who value those special moments in a natural world far away from the constant chatter and clatter and the ugly visual pollution of the urban environment. The previous Chapter gives a taste of what to expect in the Park, and the next tells you where to go and what you can see and do to experience these opportunities.

Above: The Lubungu Pontoon en route to the North-East area and Kasempa.

Below: Crinum lilies are one of the first flowering plants to appear at the start of the rains.

For the large mammal enthusiasts, come in the dry season when the grass is short and there is less browse to obstruct your viewing. Animals will also be more concentrated near sources of permanent water. However, most photographers prefer the early rainy season when the first thunderstorms have washed away the dust and brought the first flush of new

OPEN AFRICA

Open Africa aims to build conservation awareness through monitoring flagship species referring to any animal or plant in an area that is under threat, or needs more conservation attention. The species significant to the area makes it an ideal mascot for the route. By raising awareness with both the visiting tourist and the local community it is hoped that the species will benefit.

The Open Africa routes expect that the by-products from tourism will spread to local communities, enriching the lives of travellers and in the process benefitting the communities through job creation and increasing awareness of conservation and natural resource protection. Through this approach Open Africa links community tourism projects and emerging entrepreneurs with established operators to increase responsible tourism for mutual benefit. Full details on the Untamed Kafue, and other routes in Zambia can be found at www.openafrica.org

grass, flowering plants, and a spectacular greening of the landscape, which happens surprisingly quickly. At that time of the year many of the mammals will give birth as there will be more to eat and drink and milk production will be at its best. Although bird-watching is great throughout the year, it is undoubtedly even better during the rainy season when the migratory birds arrive and stay for several months.

The botanists and botanical photographers should plan their visits for the early rains when the grass is still short and when the fires are gone, a time for the burnt land to recover so amazingly quickly from ash grey to a breath-taking kaleidoscope of colours. Look out for the pink and white *Crinum* lilies and the dwarf paintbush *(Scadoxus puniceus)*, (both members of the Amaryllidaceae family), the crimson red flowers of the flame creeper *(Combretum microphyllum)*, the large globe pink flowering heard of the tumbleweed *(Boophane disticha)*, the yellow and red flowers of the flame lily *(Gloriosa superba)*, and many other flowering plants adding their brilliant colours to the verdant spring landscape.

Access to parts of KNP in the rains can be difficult and some camps are completely closed, so plan carefully to avoid disappointment. The general map of KNP and of the surrounding nine Game Management Areas (GMAs) shows the roads, tracks, entrance gates and principal wildlife viewing loops, rivers, hills, Lake Itezhi-Tezhi and locations of places to stay. We have also provided maps on geology and vegetation. The four main areas have maps that also indicate fishing areas, picnic spots and features of special interest, many of which are either under discussion or are being renovated.

SELF-DRIVE AND 4X4 EXPLORERS

KNP is fortunate in that it contains abundant opportunities for exploration and enjoyment of areas and circuits that have only recently been opened to the fast-growing 4x4 self-drive visitors' market. Routes through and around KNP are being enthusiastically developed, with *Open Africa* taking the lead (see box on page 49). The flagship species chosen for the Kafue route is the cheetah, which is viewed as a charismatic, high profile animal of great conservation significance, now being sighted throughout the Park. Conservation efforts for KNP by *Open Africa* are being extended to the wild dog, sable antelope, elephant and waterbuck. Sightings of these species will be recorded through the lodges and community campsites.

New routes are opening throughout the Park but for self-drive, high clearance 4x4 use is recommended.

One of the attractions of self-drive is the option to stop on your own to stretch your legs and have a picnic or drink, do some bird watching or recreational fishing. The designation of these fishing and picnic spots remains under discussion by the Park management and visitors should use the the main map and lists in the boxes on pages 51 and 52 as a guideline that should be checked with your lodge, camp managers or ZAWA staff if unsure of where to go. At present there are few signs for these sites but this matter is receiving active attention.

RECREATIONAL ANGLERS

For the angler the Kafue River and its tributaries offer some wonderful opportunities for spinning, fly fishing or bait casting in wild waters, a most attractive prospect by any standard. Fishing is becoming increasingly recognised as one of the Park's specialities, with rod and line light tackle, angling being permitted on licence on all the rivers and streams where fishing areas have been designated. Fishing is best in parts of the Park where there is no commercial fishing and on Lake Itezhi-Tezhi where licensed netting is permitted but is not too obtrusive. The small commercial fishery that has developed on the lake is based mainly on three species of *Tilapia* and an annual off-take of several tons of fish is being achieved.

The Kafue River and its main tributaries provide abundant opportunities for anglers especially for bream, pike and barbel.

Lake Itezhi-Tezhi has some superb fishing sites with sunsets to remember.

For anglers, knowledge of the places where fish are to be found is affected by the habitat characteristics of the lake, where there is a policy for holding water levels high during January to September which is the growing season for fish, followed by an annual drawdown. This practice seems to enable fish productivity to remain greater than in other reservoirs, such as Lake Kariba, where catches are said to have dropped considerably over the years, but monitoring of netting remains the main management concern.

Throughout the 256 km of the Kafue River where it flows through KNP, anglers have unparalleled opportunities for fishing in virtually untouched water, especially for bream, pike

FISHING AND PICNIC SITES IN THE NORTHERN SECTOR

MANAGED BY THE CHUNGA AREA MANAGEMENT UNIT BASED AT CHUNGA

Fishing sites

1. Mayukuyuku area near the camping sites on both sides of the Kafue River.
2. Lufupa, in the area around the islands and upstream of the camps.
3. Musekwa stream area around S14°34' E26°01' to S14°42 E26°06'.
4. Kafwala area along the Kafue River.
5. Hippo pool near big tree at Chunga.
6. Shishamba - Kafue confluence.
7. Lwansanza - Kafue confluence.
8. Chunga - the old pontoon area upstream from Kafumba Kwale Camp.

Picnic sites

1. Hippo pool near big tree at Chunga.
2. The old pontoon site opposite Kafumba Kwale camp.
3. Lwansanza - near the Kafue confluence.
4. The Ntemwa area near Musanza Camp.
5. Moshi area - near the Moshi airstrip and old Ranger's house.
6. Kamano area - Western Boundary.
7. Lushimba area - Western Boundary.
8. Treetops – near the Schools' Camp also known as Kondakamwale.
9. Old Kafue Pontoon training school area – near Chunga.

FISHING AND PICNIC SITES IN THE SOUTHERN SECTOR MANAGED BY THE NGOMA AREA MANAGEMENT UNIT BASED AT NGOMA
Fishing sites 1. Kunda - Musa confluence - near Lake Itezhi-Tezhi. 2. Malala confluence on west shore of Lake Itezhi-Tezhi. 3. Island 2 Musungwa - on Lake Itezhi-Tezhi. 4. Island 1 Chongo - on Lake Itezhi-Tezhi. 5. Fresher Island – on Lake Itezhi-Tezhi. 6. Lwangandu - Musa confluence – north of Lake Itezhi-Tezhi on the Spinal Road.
Picnic sites 1. Mubi pool south of Nanzhila Plains Safari Camp. 2. Zebra area - between Kalenje and Nanzhila Plains Safari Camp. 3. Sugar area - north Musa river bank. 4. Kaunga area - Western Boundary. 5. Mongosiya area – north of Lake Itezhi-Tezhi. 6. Mabiya Pool area - 18 km north of Dundumwezi Gate. 7. Dundumwezi area – in the far south. 8. Mwandu area - west of the Elephant Orphanage on the Nkala River. 9. Lwang'andu – Musa upstream from the confluence with Lake Itezhi-Tezhi.

Further information on where to fish is given in Chapter 3.

KNP fees payable by all visitors	Citizen of Zambia (ZMW)	Residents (ZMW)	SADC nationals (ZMW)	Non-residents (ZMW)
Park entrance/ adult	20,16/day	79,20/ day	79,20/day	105,60/day
School parties/ person/day Special interest Non-leisure groups	5,04/day	6,30/ day	6,30/ day	26,40/ day

and silver and black barbel, and better still you can keep your catch!

HOW TO GET THERE: ROADS; ENTRANCE GATES AND CHARGES; AIRSTRIPS

KNP can be reached comfortably on good main roads from Lusaka, Livingstone, the Copperbelt and Mongu. There are several main entry points, and those for visitor use are named for each route. Although the Park has no fences and there

The main entrance gate to Mushingashi Conservancy off the main D181 road from Mumbwa to Kasempa.

are many points where vehicles can enter, only a few are rated as main entrance gates. Park regulations require these gates to be used by visitors who must pay entrance fees for themselves and their vehicles on a daily basis. The box on page 52 shows the daily charges payable to ZAWA that apply to everyone who enters the Park in 2012, based on a four tier system with the lowest rates applicable to citizens of Zambia.

Visitors are advised to take care in choosing the route to use to get to the KNP as the roads beyond the entry points and in many cases up to the entrance, are only accessible seasonally in 4x4 vehicles with good clearance. The best tar roads lead to Nalusanga and Tateyoyo Gates – the It-zhi-

Each self-drive vehicle, boat or aircraft will be charged as follows:

Vehicle type	Locally registered (ZMW)	Foreign non-resident (ZMW)
Vehicle <3 t net wt	15,30/day	79,20/day
Vehicle >3 t net wt	25,20/day	158,40/day
Vessel < 50 hp engine	15,30/day	79,20/day
Vessel >50 hp engine	25,20/day	158,40/day
Aircraft landing in KNP	100,80/day	158,40/day
Mooring in KNP	25,20/day	158,40/day

ZAWA has also set the following daily rates for camping, boating, canoeing or rafting, and angling:

Activity	Citizens/Residents (ZMW)	Non-residents (ZMW)
Camping	18,90/day	26,40/day
Boating	31,32/day	105,60/day
Canoeing/rafting	25,20/day	105,60/day
Angling	18,90/day	26,40/day

Tezhi road is now without tar and is being gradually up-graded. The road from Kalomo to Dundumwezi is excellent gravel. Road development and maintenance is an on-going process and the conditions of roads can change, particularly after heavy rains. If you are unsure of your route, it is always wise to talk directly to your travel agent about the lodges or camps where you plan to stay (email addresses of the lodges are given at the end of this Chapter with further useful contacts in Chapter 5). There are seven main access routes to the Park to consider, two of which come from Livingstone. See the foldout map at the back of the book for further details. It is advisable to fill up with fuel before departure and again at any filling stations along the way.

Above: The M9 main road from Lusaka to KNP and Mongu at the twin baobabs landmark en route to Mumbwa.

1. *From Lusaka*: The M9 Highway is a first class tar road. It takes two hours or less to reach the Nalusanga Entrance Gate (open all year) via Mumbwa.

2. *From Livingstone*: Two options available. (i) Take the T1 highway northwards to Kalomo, turning off by the Kobil petrol station, and following the route north-westwards through the open air market to the newly up-graded D710 gravel road to the Dundumwezi Entrance Gate, a two hour drive from Livingstone to the gate. Dundumwezi is open all year round but a high clearance 4x4 is needed at present beyond the gate. (ii) Take the Kasungula main road westwards out of Livingstone and then after about 129 km turn north at the Simungoma junction up to Mulobezi township (97 km) and from there on to the Park boundary and Old Barotse Cattle Cordon road at the Kalumbu Entrance which is simply a T-junction at the moment.

Below: Dundumwezi Entrance Gate that was built in 2011 to replace one that had been used from the time the Park was first opened to the public in 1958.

The Kafue River provides many outstanding opportunities for picnic and fishing spots.

3. *From the Copperbelt to the north of KNP*: Travel to the northwestern provincial capital of Solwezi and then due south to Kasempa, continuing on southwards to the Kabanga Entrance Gate north of the Busanga Plain. Once through the gate this becomes a rough sandy gravel road that is graded in the dry season and accessible by 4x4 vehicles only. It is advisable to check on the condition before departure. The journey can take up to four hours. As

PLANNING YOUR TRIP TO KNP: distances in kilometres

From:	To:	Approximate distance (km)
Kitwe	Kabanga Gate via Kasempa	432
Ndola	Nalusanga Gate via Lusaka	399
Kabwe	Nalusanga Gate via Lusaka	222
Lusaka	Itezhi-Tezhi Dam	334
Mongu M9	Tateyoyo Gate	255
Monze	Namwala	142
Livingstone T1	Kalomo	120
Kalomo	Dundumwezi Gate	74
Lusaka M9	Mumbwa	145
Mumbwa M9	Nalusanga Gate	38
Mumbwa	Itezhi-Tezhi turning	65
M9 Highway turning	Itezhi-Tezhi Dam Wall	124
Itezhi-Tezhi Dam Wall	Musa Gate	6
Livingstone M10	Mulobezi turning (Simungoma)	97
Simungoma M10	Kalumbu/ Cordon Rd	198

an alternative (see map) the Masozhi Gate gives access to the Busanga Plain from the north. It is a rough sandy road restricted to dry season use and 4x4 vehicles only.

4. *From Mongu across the central part of KNP*: Travel due east from Mongu along the M9 Highway on tar to the Tateyoyo Entrance Gate (open all year) and less than a three-hour drive. Where a 4x4 vehicle is required inside the Park, this is mentioned under lodge descriptions.

5. *From Namwala to Ngoma and Itezhi-Tezhi*: This is a rough 60 km sandy track across the wide grassy plains of the Kafue Flats. It is not open in the rainy season. The journey requires a 4x4 and can take at least two hours to reach the Nakalomwe Entrance Gate (under repair) near Ngoma, passing Chief Musungwa's Palace on the way. The Itezhi-Tezhi Musa Entrance Gate gives access to Ngoma and the lake. It is a rough surfaced road but accessible all year round as far as Ngoma and to Ngoma airstrip. In the rains it is usually possible to reach Nanzhila further south by 4x4 via the Cordon Road.

6. *From Mumbwa to the north-east*: Take the rough gravel road immediately past the Total filling station (first left from the roundabout coming from Lusaka) and follow

Red lechwe in the far north of the KNP are a special attraction of this remote area.

the recently upgraded gravel road marked to Kasempa. The new Chalanta Entrance Gate is a joint venture between ZAWA and the Mushingashi Conservancy on the Mumbwa to Kasempa road D181 and is located 13 km before the Mushingashi Entrance and south of Kabulushi.

There is one additional important well-signposted Entrance Gate situated near the Kafue Hook Bridge on the Spinal Road due north off the M9 Highway. This is in use in the dry season only, but improvement to an all-weather condition is on-going. Visitors should enquire about road conditions when checking in.

The following key waypoints will help to plan overland

Monze to Ngoma via Namwala		
Monze Town	S16°16'914"	E27°28'775"
Namwala Town	S15°45'259"	E26°25'523"
Musa Entrance Gate	S15°47'800"	E25°59'934"
Southern Area HQ Ngoma	S15°54'658"	E25°57'156"

Livingstone to Ngoma via Mulobezi & Nanzhila Plains Safari Camp		
Livingstone Town (ENGEN fuel station)	S17°52'187"	E25°51'347"
Simungoma turning	S17°24'567"	E24°39'056"
Machili Village	S16°50'457"	E25°06'702"
Mulobezi Sawmill	S16°46'798"	E25°10'469"
Mulanga ZAWA Entrance Gate	S16°55'222"	E25°17'602"
Kalumbu D714 junction	S16°33'886"	E25°42'349"
Nanzhila Plains Safari Camp	S16°16'465"	E25°55'51[illegible]"
Ngoma aerodrome	S15°57'939"	E25°56'38[illegible]"
Southern Area HQ Ngoma	S15°54'658"	E25°57'156"

All ZAWA CHARGES are subject to change without notice and it is advisable to check these in the ZAWA website: www.zawa.org

Above: Ngoma all-weather airstrip.

travel for two of the routes to and within the area. Further details on how to access all the camps and lodges are given in Chapter 3.

Airstrips: There are eight airstrips of varying quality that provide access to the KNP but only those at Ngoma (capable of taking planes up to the size of a HS 748), Chunga, Lufupa and Hippo Lodge can be considered as all-weather. Airstrips at Lufupa, Puku Pan, Lushimba Outpost, Busanga and Lunga River Lodge are seasonal. An airstrip is being developed at Nanzhila Plains Safari Camp and should be open by 2013. All those listed above are open to charter flights. At present KNP has no scheduled commercial flights, but this could change as tourism develops. Applications for private landings at all airstrips should be made to

Below: A wide levee and landward floodplain on the bank of the Kafue River that permits a line of riverine vegetation along most of the upper and middle stretches of the river.

Accommodation options in the KNP

Lodge:	Accommodation in permanent structures with catering and a wide range of tourist facilities.
Camp:	Accommodation and facilities as for a lodge but constructed mainly in semi-permanent materials.
Bush Camp:	Constructed on a seasonal or permanent site using tented or bush poles and grass structures.
Fly-Camp:	Not on a permanent site and only using tents for accommodation; usually temporary arrangements made by lodges or camps for their clients only.
Campsite:	Located at a permanent site with an agreed number of stands, served by permanent showers, toilets and kitchen facilities.

the Director General, Zambia Wildlife Authority, Private Bag 1, Chilanga: Phone: +260.21.127-8525. We recommend that you plan your flights well in advance as these applications can be very time-consuming.

WHERE TO STAY

In 2012, there were 34 accommodation options available for visitor use in and around the Park, ranging from sophisticated up-market lodges, to basic camping facilities. They vary greatly in standard and cost. Chapter 3 provides detailed information on their locations, the type of accommodation and what to see and do. Rather than ranking them by hotel-style star classes, they have been rated by price bands “a – f” since price usually (not always) defines the standard of accommodation and range of facilities available. All are listed for easy reference in Ready Reference on Where to Stay on pages 61 to 64 at the end of this Chapter. The list tells you whether the lodge or camp is open throughout the year or not and also gives you the GPS waypoints, the website if

Nanzhila Plains Safari Camp.

available, and a contact email or phone number for bookings.

The services and their additional charges vary from lodge to lodge. Visitors should ascertain exactly what is provided over and above the overnight stay (and full catering when specified) for activities such as safari drives, night drives, escorted walking, river and lake trips, etc., and these should all be confirmed at the time the booking is made. As items like park fees, road conditions, lodge information, etc. are subject to fairly regular changes, all visitors are advised to check the website, www.kafuetrust.org, for the latest information, and to check with the lodges themselves for any "special offers" that might be available.

Price bands in US$ per person per night for KNP accommodation options	
25 - 50	a
51 - 100	b
101 - 150	c
151 - 250	d
251 - 500	e
501 -1,000 plus	f

READY REFERENCE ON WHERE TO STAY

Name of Lodge or Camp	**Style**	**Number of beds**	**Operator contact**
Busanga Bush Camp	Bush Camp	8	zambia@wilderness.co.zm www.wilderness-safaris.com
Chibila Camp (WECSZ)	Camp	12	wecsz@zamnet.zm www.conservationzambia.org
Chunga Camp	Camp	12 (4)	nexim@zamnet.zm
Delai Camp	Bush Camp	8	darrell@mushingashi.co.zm www.mushingashi.net
Heron Camp (under re-construction)	Camp	20 (5)	jm.wessels@hotmail.com
Hippo Lodge	Lodge	16	hippolodge@zamnet.zm www.hippolodge.com
Hornbill Lodge (Mumbuluma)	Lodge	8	info@mumbuluma.com www.mumbuluma.com
Kafue River Camp	Camp	8 (5)	kafueriver@iwayafrica.com www.kafueriver.com
Kafumba Kwale	Bush Camp	8 (6)	mutemwachambers@iconnect.zm
Kafwala Camp (WECSZ)	Camp	8	wecsz@zamnet.zm www.conservationzambia.org
Kaingu Safari Lodge	Lodge	12	info@kaingu-lodge.com www.kaingu-lodge.com
Kalonga Waloba Camp	Camp	24	darrell@mushingashi.co.zm www.mushingashi.net
Kapalause Cottage Guest House	Lodge	8	darrell@mushingashi.co.zm www.mushingashi.net
Kapinga Bush Camp	Bush Camp	8	zambia@wilderness.co.zm www.wilderness-safaris.com
Kashikoto Camp	Bush Camp	10	darrell@mushingashi.co.zm www.mushingashi.net
Konkamoya Lodge with Hippo Bay Campsite	Lodge	10 (6)	bwanasafari@gmail.com info@konkamoya.com www.konkamoya.com
Leopard Lodge	Lodge	12	info@leopard-lodge.com www.leopard-lodge.com
Lufupa Bush Camp	Camp	16	zambia@wilderness.co.zm www.wilderness-safaris.com
Lufupa River Camp	Lodge	18 (10)	zambia@wilderness.co.zm www.wilderness-safaris.com

READY REFERENCE ON WHERE TO STAY

Location k/GMA/Pvt	Seasonal or Year-round	Full Catering (F) Self Catering (SC)	Price range	GPS Waypoint
Park	Seasonal	F	(f)	S14°12'800" E25°51'184"
GMA	Year-round	SC	(a)	S15°46'639" E26°00'406"
Park	Year-round	SC	(a)	S15°02'560" E26°00'003"
Pvt	Year-round	SC	(a)	S14°28'324" E26°38'576"
GMA	Year-round	SC	(a)	S14°57'893" E25°58'424"
Park	Year-round	F	(d/e)	S14°40'623" E26°22'530"
Park	Seasonal	F	(f)	S16°11'925" E26°01'891"
GMA	Seasonal	F	(c)	S14°29'841" E26°31'206"
GMA	Seasonal	SC	(a)	S15°02'254" E26°02'214"
Park	Seasonal	SC	(a)	S14°47'853" E26°11'068"
GMA	Year-round	F	(d)	S15°17'817" E25°58'720"
Pvt	Year-round	SC	(a)	S14°27'091" E26°38'276"
Pvt	Year-round	SC	(a)	S14°27'500" E26°41'160"
Park	Seasonal	F	(f)	S14°12'661" E25°48'976"
Pvt	Year-round	SC	(a)	S14°27'336" E26°34'550"
Park	Seasonal	F	(e)	S15°52'054" E25°52'980"
GMA	Seasonal	F	(d/e)	S14°32'513" E26°28'591"
Park	Seasonal	F	(d)	S14°48'113" E26°11'178"
Park	Seasonal	F	(d)	S14°36'996" E26°11'478"

READY REFERENCE ON WHERE TO STAY

Name of Lodge or Camp	Style	Number of beds	Operator contact
Lufupa Tented Camp	Bush Camp	18	zambia@wilderness.co.zm www.wilderness-safaris.com
Lunga River Lodge	Lodge	12	rzw@iconnect.zm
Mayukuyuku Bush Camp	Bush Camp	4 (5)	kafuecamps@btinternet.com www.kafuecamps.com
McBrides' Camp	Bush Camp	16 (5)	McBrides.Camp@uuplus.net www.mcbridescamp.com
Mukambi Safari Lodge	Lodge	24 (5)	info@mukambi.com www.mukambi.com
Mukombo Lodge	Lodge	20 (6)	mushitu@yahoo.co.uk
Musanza Tented Camp	Bush Camp	12	zambia@wilderness.co.zm www.wilderness-safaris.com
Musungwa Lodge	Lodge	72	zamker@zamnet.zm www.musungwalodge.co.za
Nanzhila Plains Safari Camp	Lodge	12 (4)	info@nanzhila.com www.nanzhila.com
New Kalala Camp	Lodge	12 (6)	info@newkalala.com www.newkalala.com
Plains Camp Busanga	Bush Camp	8	info@mukambi.com www.mukambi.com
Puku Pan Safari Lodge	Lodge	16 (8)	pukupan@zamnet.zm www.pukupan.com
Shumba Bush Camp	Bush Camp	8	zambia@wilderness.co.zm www.wilderness-safaris.com
Treetops Schools' Camp (Kondakamwale)	Camp	36	treetopsschoolscamp@gmail.com www.treetopskafue.webs.com
Zamlodge – Amarula Camp	Camp	5 (6)	djohnbolton@gmail.com info@zamlodge.com

The second figure in brackets under "Beds" indicates the number of camping stands. GMA = Game Management Area. Bold type indicates the presence of a "Hub". These are well-established lodges and camps that in many ways act as gateways to their parts of KNP.

READY REFERENCE ON WHERE TO STAY				
Location rk/GMA/Pvt	**Seasonal or Year-round**	**Full Catering (F) Self Catering (SC)**	**Price range**	**GPS Waypoint**
Park	Seasonal	F	(e)	S14°36'941" E26°11'403"
GMA	Seasonal	F	(d)	S14°11'600" E26°21'500"
Park	Year-round	F/SC	(a/d)	S14°54'989" E26°03'913"
Park	Year-round	F	(d/e)	S14°41'542" E26°23'110"
GMA	Year-round	F	(d)	S14°58'611" E25°59'532"
Park	Seasonal	F	(b/c)	S14°54'190" E26°02'350"
Park	Seasonal	F	(e)	S14°23'184 E26°02'054"
GMA	Year-round	F	(c)	S15°47'00" E26°00'19"
Park	Seasonal	F	(d)	S16°16'465" E25°55'510"
GMA	Year-round	F	(c)	S15°46'186" E26°00'862"
Park	Seasonal	F	(e)	S14°10'830" E25°49'165"
GMA	Seasonal	F	(c)	S15°12'836" E25°58'675"
Park	Seasonal	F	(f)	S14°13'159" E25°52'350"
Park	Seasonal	SC	(a)	S14°24'232" E26°02'503"
Park	Year-round	SC	(a)	S14°54' 743" E26°06'235"

Since the lodges and camps are being continually developed, please be aware that some of the details above may change without notice.

WHERE TO GO AND WHAT TO SEE AND DO

Apart from the Nalusanga to Tateyoyo M9 Highway road, there are no tarred roads in the Park. All other roads are unsurfaced, generally only passable for high clearance 4x4 vehicles and are usually open between May to November inclusive, depending on the start, duration and intensity of the rains. The tourism season at times is longer and at other times, especially in the extreme north and south of the Park, where clay soils predominate, much shorter. It is advisable to check this with your travel agent or with ZAWA, the ZTB or KPOA lodge owners and operators.

Visitors must stay on the graded roads and must not leave their cars, except at approved places such as lodges, fishing spots and picnic sites. Speed limits are 40 km/h on connecting roads and 25 km/h on loops. Driving after dark is not permitted, but night drives can be arranged by licensed lodge managers or through ZAWA.

Waypoints for lodges and key junctions have been added to the text to support the descriptions of routes and options that you can find along the way for where to go, what there is to see and what to do. Every effort has been made to make them as accurate as possible within a range of a few metres. Please note that many of the place names vary between publications. Names that are presently being used by ZAWA have been preferred throughout this Guide. To facilitate planning your visit to such a vast part of Zambia, KNP has been divided into four areas shown on the Map on the right, namely (i) North-East, (ii) North-West, (iii) Central and (iv) Southern.

KNP has been divided into four areas to facilitate visitor planning.

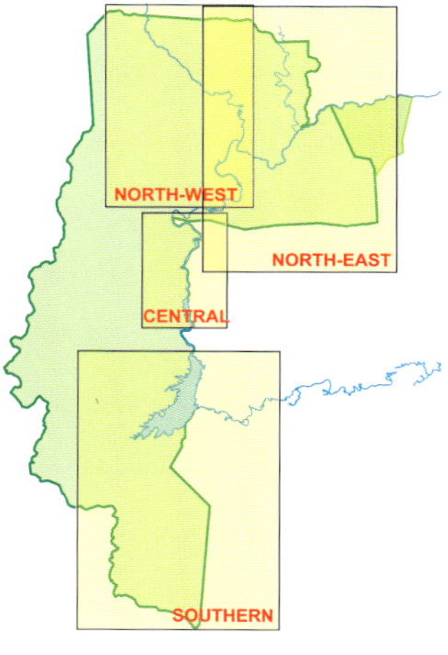

PLACES TO STAY IN THE NORTH-EAST

Mayukweyukwe Area
Mayukuyuku Bush Camp
Mukombo Safari Lodge
Zamlodge - Amarula Camp

Hippo Mine-Mushingashi-Lubungu Area
Hippo Safari Lodge
Kafue River Camp
Leopard Lodge
Lunga River Lodge
McBrides' Camp
Delai Camp
Kalonga Waloba Camp
Kapalause Cottage Guest House
Kashikoto Camp

On the journey from Lusaka to the northern parts of KNP, respect the 80/km signs and look out for the following on the M9 highway:

- 42 km: the Mwembeshi Earth Station (Zambia's first satellite communications complex).
- 50 km: an interesting relic patch of mopane woodland (the nearest to Lusaka).
- 97 km: the large twin baobab trees that flank the road.
- 123 km: the Dunavant Cotton Ginnery.
- 145 km: Mumbwa Town, an old colonial district headquarters and a single street of "local-style" shops, a market for all kinds of local produce and a bus station. Places to stay or take a break include the Mumbwa Motel, Kalundu Motel and the refurbished New La Hacienda Hotel.

NORTH-EAST AREA

For the purposes of this Guide, the North-East Area has been demarcated as a relatively new and important development for the KNP. It is situated to the north of the M9 Highway and to the east of the Kafue River, and is gradually becoming much better known these days on account of improvements to the access roads and easily reachable attractive places to stay, which offer a range of opportunities for all kinds of safari interests, different types of accommodation, week-end trips and a good spread of costs and activities. The North-East has two clusters of accommodation. On the western side near the Kafue Hook Bridge is the Mayukweyukwe Area, easily reached from the excellent tar road from Lusaka through Mumbwa and then on through the Nalusanga Entrance Gate (S14°58'275" E26°42'699"). This has a swing bar across the road and a small and ancient green kiosk set some way off the road to the right, but this is now being replaced by a new modern structure. On the opposite side is a growing traditional market where local produce is actively and cheerfully traded. You will be asked to fill in the entrance

Roads and camps in the North-East Area.

register by ZAWA gate staff and it is here that you can enquire about the next step of your journey if you feel at all unsure about the road ahead. Turn off on an access road to the Mayukweyukwe Area is on the right at S14°57'742" E26°05'541" just before the Kafue Hook Bridge.

Diametrically to the north-east (the Hippo Mine-Mushingashi-Lubungu Area) is accessed by leaving the tar road and turning left at the first roundabout and filling station in Mumbwa where, after a short stretch of rough road that crosses the Mushingashi River, a good, newly improved gravel road to Kasempa, the D181, will take you to the new Chalanta Entrance Gate at S14°43'139" E26°47'186" and on into the KNP itself. From there on, carefully follow the signs to the camps. The Lunga River Lodge is in the north of this area on its own and can be reached by continuing on the D181 and turning westwards to join a marked bush track that leads south-eastwards to the camp on the bank of the Lunga River (one of the major tributaries of the Kafue). If your destination is the Mushingashi Conservancy, look out for the well-signposted turning on your right off the Kasempa road 13 km after the Chalanta Gate, which will take you to an entry kiosk set a little way back from the road. The turning to Hippo Lodge, McBride's camp and Hippo Mine is 23 km after Kabulushi gate at a sharp bend where you turn left.

Mushingashi-ZAWA Chalanta entrance gate 13 km from the main entrance to Mushingashi Conservancy on the Mumbwa to Kasempa D181 main road.

WHAT TO SEE AND DO IN THE MAYUKWEYUKWE AREA					
Lodge/camp name	***Wildlife viewing***	***Boating***	***Fishing***	***Birding***	***Walking trails***
Mayukuyuku Bush Camp	+	+	+	+	+
Mukombo Safari Lodge	+	+	+	+	+
Zamlodge–Amarula Camp	+	+	+	+	

MAYUKWEYUKWE AREA

Along the entire stretch of road from the Nalusanga Entrance Gate to the Kafue Hook Bridge, the Park is on the right (the north) and the Mumbwa Game Management Area on the left. The woodland is relatively undamaged miombo, and is intersected by small river crossings and long grassy dambos with occasional sightings of sable antelope, hartebeest, buffalo, warthog and reedbuck. As the road slopes gradually towards the Kafue River and the turning on the right to Zamlodge, Mukombo and Mayukuyuku camps, more frequent sightings will be made of puku, impala, zebra, warthog and baboon and sometimes hartebeest and sable antelope, often very close to the road.

Early morning mist on the Kafue River heralds the start of another great day in the Park.

Mayukuyuku Bush Camp:
S14°54'989" E26°03'913"

This is a well-established, all-year-round camping site with plenty of space in an attractive riverside setting midst tall trees, opposite a large pool just downstream of tree-clad islands with rapids passing between rounded, water-eroded rocks. It is a most attractive and quiet environment for camping at five well-spaced camping stands with summer shelters. There are also four large, double tents with ensuite H&C showers and toilets. Mayukuyuku has two thatched bar areas and a dining room with adjacent barbecue, close to the water's edge. The reception at the camp, outstandingly managed by Patrick Moyo, is always friendly, helpful and well informed on river conditions, the wildlife situation, bird watching and fishing. Whilst the camp is set up mainly for self-drive travellers and week-enders, it also offers escorted safari drives, boat trips and guided walks in the immediate vicinity or elsewhere in the KNP or in the Mumbwa Management Area. For those who do not want to cater for themselves, the Camp offers simple dining with an emphasis on Zambian meat and fish, fresh vegetables, fruits, salads and homemade soups.

See *www.kafuecamps.com* for further information. For bookings contact Pippa Turner at *kafuecamps@btinternet.com* or *info@kafuecamps.com* or phone +260.977.721-284.

Mukombo Lodge:
S14°54'190"
E26°02'350"

This comparatively new class *(b-c)* safari lodge is built on the riverbank overlooking a wide stretch of water with attractive riverine vegetation flanking it on both banks. Mukombo is built in traditional thatched style with small windows and no verandas. There are three double chalets and two single chalets, all ensuite with H&C showers and toilets. The camp has a bar and dining room with a good view to the river. Self-drive camping is also offered.

For bookings contact Phylllis Simasiku at *mushitu@yahoo.co.uk* or phone +260.211.226-082

Zamlodge - Amarula Camp:
S14°97'694" E25°99'286"

The camp is set in riparian woodland stretching down to the river's edge, and although it was still under construction early in 2012, it already offers five simple thatched chalets with double and single beds, a basic dining room, six camping stands with barbecues situated close to the chalets, and communal toilets and showers with H&C water.

For bookings contact Dennis Bolton at *djohnbolton@gmail.com* or phone +260.211.295-204; mobile +260.97.784-9403.

WHAT TO SEE AND DO IN THE HIPPO MINE-MUSHINGASHI-LUBUNGU AREA

Lodge/camp name	*Wildlife viewing*	*Boating*	*Fishing*	*Birding*	*Walking trails*	*Hot Springs*
Hippo Lodge	+	+	+	+	+	–
Kafue River Camp	+	+	+	+	+	–
Leopard Lodge	+	+	+	+	+	+
Lunga River Lodge	+	+	+	+	+	
McBrides' Camp	+	+	+	+	+	

Hippo Mine-Mushingashi-Lubungu Area

This part of the Park is noted for varied terrain and diversity of habitats, especially unspoilt riparian woodland, dambos with reeds and papyrus that retain water during the dry season, miombo woodland with an under-storey, and dense deciduous thickets and wooded islands where bush fires seldom occur. These provide good viewing of large mammals, especially elephant, roan, sable, hartebeest, reedbuck, leopard and lion and rarities such as blue and yellow-backed duiker and sitatunga. Crocodile, hippo and elephant are seen regularly at close range on guided boat trips along the river that improve as the dry season progresses. At night the haunting sounds of lion and hyaena are often heard.

This area gets its name from the old Hippo Mine, which was the first copper mine in Zambia north of the Zambezi established in 1897 and its history is steeped in triumph and disaster that have never been properly researched and presented to the outside world. It forms part of the wonderful fabric of Zambia's cultural heritage (see box).

The area is building up a deserved reputation as one of the best catalogued for birding in Zambia. About 300 species have been recorded in the locality, including the African finfoot, African skimmer, Böhm's bee-eater, rock pratincole, crowned and wattled crane, saddle-billed stork, racket-tailed roller, Sharlow's turaco, Ross's turaco, Pel's fishing owl, crowned eagle that nest nearby, and the African fish-eagle.

Hippo Lodge: S14°40'623" E26°22'530"

This is one of the first private lodges to be built in the Park. It started its life as a traditional bush camp with structures made of rustic local materials situated very close to the Kafue River. It is now a stylish, well-established lodge with permanent chalets and excellent visitor facilities that cater for self-drive clients and groups. The riverside lodge 2km from Hippo airstrip, in price bracket *(d-f)* has evolved over many years and has gradually raised standards of accommodation and service to become a first class base and hub for safaris in the north-eastern part of the Park. It has a beautiful, tranquil location set neatly on a wide part of the river with over 70 km of navigable waterways for boating, wildlife watching, birding and fishing. The Lodge has four ensuite stone and thatch chalets built in thatched "vintage-style", each with a veranda looking across the river. Adjacent to these there are two large safari tents with attached open-air stone bathrooms.

- *Honeymoon house,* that has been recently refurbished, is designed for comfort and privacy and is set under large jackal berry trees very close to the riverbank.
- *Munjili House* is a small family chalet and ideal for bird watching, set back from the river with great views of the bush. (*Munjili* means warthog in the local language).
- *Imberbe House* is a large, thatched, A-frame structure lodged neatly between two large

HIPPO MINE

The old mine workings, relic equipment and original buildings stand stark today as a true marker of the endeavour of early explorers, geologists and hard workers who faced the physical and psychological challenges of a land without infrastructure, dangerous animals, no health facilities, inadequate transport and communications and scanty market information, which today are readily available and taken for granted.

The open mine pit has left a long, deep channel on the landscape and the remnants of the machinery for the underground workings remain as an evocative, somewhat sombre monument to all the human endeavour that went into extraction of copper ore in this remote place.

An aspect of respect and pathos for the pioneer workers is the memorial plaque that reads:
Henry (1920-2007)
Martha (1919 - 2008)
Oosthuizen "Loved this place" *and the grave of Vivian Allison the manager who died in a tragic accident at the mine.*

leadwood trees *(Combretum imberbe)*, hence the name.

- *Stony House* is spacious and organised to accommodate self-catering families and small special-interest safari groups for up to six people. It has its own kitchen, laundry service and domestic staff. Guests can also make use of the full-board option at the prevailing daily rate.

There is a shady bar adjacent to the dining room, both facing the river. A swimming pool and barbecue area are located nearby. A cluster of hot springs is situated about a kilometre from the lodge. For those who would like to take a dip in the warm, clear water, bathing at the spring is a popular activity.

See
www.hippolodge.com
for further information.
Contact Mirjana Boltar
by email to make
reservations and
enquiries at
hippolodge@zamnet.zm
or phone
+260.978.877-388 or
+260.211.295-298, or
+260.977.788-910.

Kafue River Camp:
S14°29'841" E26°31'206"

This is a much-loved, traditional canvas and thatch camp, *(e)* class, with large ensuite tents on concrete foundations arranged close to an attractive stretch on the Kafue River. Teak decking overlooks the river, providing views along the river and across to the Park on the opposite bank. There are five large ensuite thatched tented chalets set on permanent foundations under high trees on the Kafue River bank. There is a dining room with full catering facilities, and a fully-equipped kitchen for self-catering guests. Kafue Camp also has a self-catering camping site with five stands with river frontage and with two ablution blocks and H&C water. Barbecue area and firewood provided. Fishing from the land or by boat is a serious speciality, with fishing permits provided at the camp. The best time is late in the dry season.

See *www.kafueriver.com* for further information. For bookings contact *kafueriver@iwayafrica.com* or phone +260.977.933-000.

Leopard Lodge: S14°32'513" E26°28'591"

The well-constructed, family-run lodge, *(e)* class, is thoughtfully situated amongst riparian vegetation on the bank of the Kafue River in the Lunga-Luswishi Game Management Area just north of the Lubungu Pontoon on the north-eastern boundary of the Park. The area around the lodge includes some good areas for wildlife viewing and the Chipushi Hot Spring. There are five twin-bedded ensuite, thatched, traditional safari lodge-style chalets, and a dining room and bar. For self-catering campers, there are also six stands in a serviced camping site. In addition to the full range activities in the area, the lodge will also arrange excursions to a nearby village for an authentic cultural experience.

See *www.leopard-lodge.com* for further information. For bookings contact Jacques Collins at *info@leopard-lodge.com* or phone +27.82.416-5894.

Lunga River Lodge:
S14°11'600" E26°21'500"

This is a well-established, high class *(e-f),* riverside, traditional safari lodge that sets outstandingly high standards of accommodation and service. Pre-booking is essential. A maximum of 12 guests can be accommodated in six spacious thatched rooms, ensuite with both bath and shower and private decks that overlook the Lunga River. There is a bar with sundeck that is suspended over the river, a dining room and deck, reading room and plunge pool. A steam room and massage facilities are also on offer. The lodge has its own airstrip at S14°11'00" E26°21'00". This is the most northerly camp in the North-East Area, and in both the Lunga-Luswishi Game Management Area, where it is located, and in the Park nearby, visitors are always impressed by the good wildlife viewing, bird watching and fishing.

> For bookings contact Doug Reynolds or Emma Wood at *rzw@iconnect.zm* or phone +260.97.853-2744

McBrides' Camp:
S14°41'542" E26°23'110"

This is a truly rustic safari camp neatly kept in traditional pole and thatch style, *(d/e)* price, owned and managed by Chris McBride of the White Lions of Timbavati fame and his wife Charlotte, who have lived all their lives in the bush and have an intimate knowledge of the

camp area and of all the wildlife to be found there. The camp has seven twin-bedded ensuite chalets with H&C water, toilet and shower, and also an independent campsite for self-drive visitors, with stands for five vehicles and two ablution blocks with toilets, H&C showers and basins. Meals are available at the main camp on request. A fly (seasonal) bush camp is being developed for a maximum of six frame tents 14 km from the main camp and is reached by boat or an 8 km walk. Temporary overnight fly-camps are also planned on a five-day bush trail route in an area where species such as buffalo and lion are often to be found. This new camping and walking opportunity with the McBrides brings you about as close to nature as is possible these days. Although the camp is open throughout the year, visitors should contact the camp to confirm the best route once the rains have started.

See *www.mcbridescamp.com* for further information. For bookings contact Chris and Charlotte McBride at *McBrides.Camp@uuplus.net* or phone +260.97.741-4871, or Skype *christopher.james.mcbride*

MUSHINGASHI CONSERVANCY

The unfenced private land of the Mushingashi Conservancy covers 38,000 ha, and lies immediately to the east of the Park boundary and along attractive stretches of the Kafue River. It is part of what was once called the "Big Concession", an amalgamation of prospecting areas and farms that were joined together in 1902 in what remains a very wild area despite some attempts at agriculture and cattle ranching. The Conservancy is developing a reputation for exceptionally effective management by Darrell Watt, whose home is there, and for abundant wildlife, boating and fishing, and is open throughout the year. It offers five different self-catering places to stay in the price bracket (a) and all the camps are delightfully located on the banks of the Kafue. The entire area is set in different types of miombo and riparian woodland, interspersed by dambos, small floodplains and dense thickets. Wildlife viewing along the 500 km of bush tracks is outstanding, including most large mammals, such as sable and roan antelope, hartebeest, reedbuck, puku, buffalo, leopard and lion, and specials include uncommon species such as sitatunga and blue and yellow-backed duiker. Visits to the Piamanzi hot springs can be arranged, S14°29'757" E26°42'164", where there is also mobile phone connectivity. The main office for the Conservancy is at S14°27'623" E26°41'232" at Kapalause.

Miombo woodland in spring flush.

Kapalause Cottage Guest House: S14°27'500" E26°14'160"

The guesthouse is located on the eastern side of the Conservancy near the Managing Director's house and overlooking a wonderful wide stretch on a bend of the Kafue River with an extensive grassy floodplain on the opposite side, where puku, reedbuck and sitatunga are to be seen. It is fully set up for families of up to eight on a self-catering but serviced basis, including a highly experienced chef.

WHAT TO SEE AND DO IN THE MUSHINGASHI CONSERVANCY					
Lodge/camp name	***Wildlife viewing***	***Boating***	***Fishing***	***Birding***	***Walking trails***
Kapalause Cottage Guest House	+	+	+	+	+
Kalonga Waloba Camp	+	+	+	+	+
Delai Camp with nearby campsite	+	+	+	+	+
Kashikoto Camp	+		+	+	+

Kalonga Waloba Camp: S14°27'091" E26°38'276"

This is the main Mushingashi camp situated on the Kafue River bank, overlooking an attractive stretch of the river where sunsets, moonlight reflections off the river and early morning mists can be breath-taking and where fishing for pike, bream and barbel is often outstanding. There is a resident cook and a dining room, and there are 14 comfortable ensuite serviced chalets each with a veranda.

Delai Camp: S14°28'324" E26°38'576"

Situated on a grassy bank by the Kafue River overlooking a wide stretch upstream where there is a group of wooded islands. The camp has six traditional thatched chalets, twin-bedded, ensuite H&C shower and toilet, and there is a bar, dining room, camp fire and barbecue area.

Between Delai and Kalonga Waloba Camps in a remote woodland area there is a *serviced camping* site with seven stands and separate H&C showers, toilets and barbecue facilities with firewood available. Arrangements can be made at Delai for the services of a cook and helper. No accommodation facilities are provided.

Kashikoto Camp: S14°27'336" E26°34'550"

The camp is close to the KNP boundary on the extreme west side of the Mushingashi Conservancy, and is set in mature riverine woodland on the banks of the Kafue River. This is a most attractive site with wide expanses of open water opposite the camp, and with rushing water upstream between the islands in the river. Kashikoto can accommodate up to 14 guests in their six traditional thatched chalets with ensuite H&C shower and toilet, and there is a bar and dining room, camp fire and barbecue area.

See *www.mushingashi.net* for further information on the Conservancy and all of its camps. For bookings contact Darrell Watt at *darrellwatt@yahoo.com* or *darrellwatt7@gmail.com* or phone +260.97.784-6978

WHAT TO SEE AND DO IN THE SOUTHERN PART OF THE NORTH-WEST AREA						
Lodge/camp name	***Wildlife viewing***	***Boating***	***Fishing***	***Birding***	***Walking trails***	***Hot Air Ballooning***
Lufupa Bush Camp	+	+	+	+	+	
Kafwala Camp (WECSZ)	+	+	+	+		
Lufupa River Camp	+	+	+	+	+	+
Lufupa Tented Camp	+	+	+	+	+	+
Treetops Schools Camp: Reserved for schools groups on educational programmes						

PLACES TO STAY IN THE NORTH-WEST

Southern part
Lufupa Bush Camp
Kafwala Camp (WECSZ)
Lufupa River Camp
Lufupa Tented Camp
Treetops Schools Camp
Busanga Plain
Musanza Tented Camp
Shumba Bush Camp
Kapinga Bush Camp
Busanga Bush Camp
Plains Camp, Busanga

NORTH-WEST AREA

Coming from Lusaka, the well-signposted road to the North-West joins the M9 Highway soon after you cross the Hook Bridge at the northern Hook Bridge Entrance Gate at S14°56'594" E25°54'369". Whilst the Spinal Road to the north is regularly maintained and follows a well-defined route, the tracks around and on the Busanga Plain and the wildlife viewing loops elsewhere, are sometimes liable to adjustment and there are few signposts so that it is important to enquire about this in advance or at least at the place you intend to stay where sketch maps of the loops are usually available. There are no self-drive camping facilities available at present in this whole area within the Park. Seasonality remains the main constraint to tourism here and this too should be considered when you are planning your trip on account of the lack of all-weather roads and viewing loops. Additional access to the area is available through the Tateyoyo and Kabanga Entrance Gates (see Chapter 2).

This part of the KNP is best known for the magnificent Busanga Plain and its marvellous opportunities for wildlife viewing, supplemented by some equally attractive country and excellent wildlife viewing along the tributaries that lead from the area to the Kafue River, notably the Ntemwa and Lufupa Rivers. For the purposes of this Guide, the North-West of KNP has been divided into these two main focal areas:

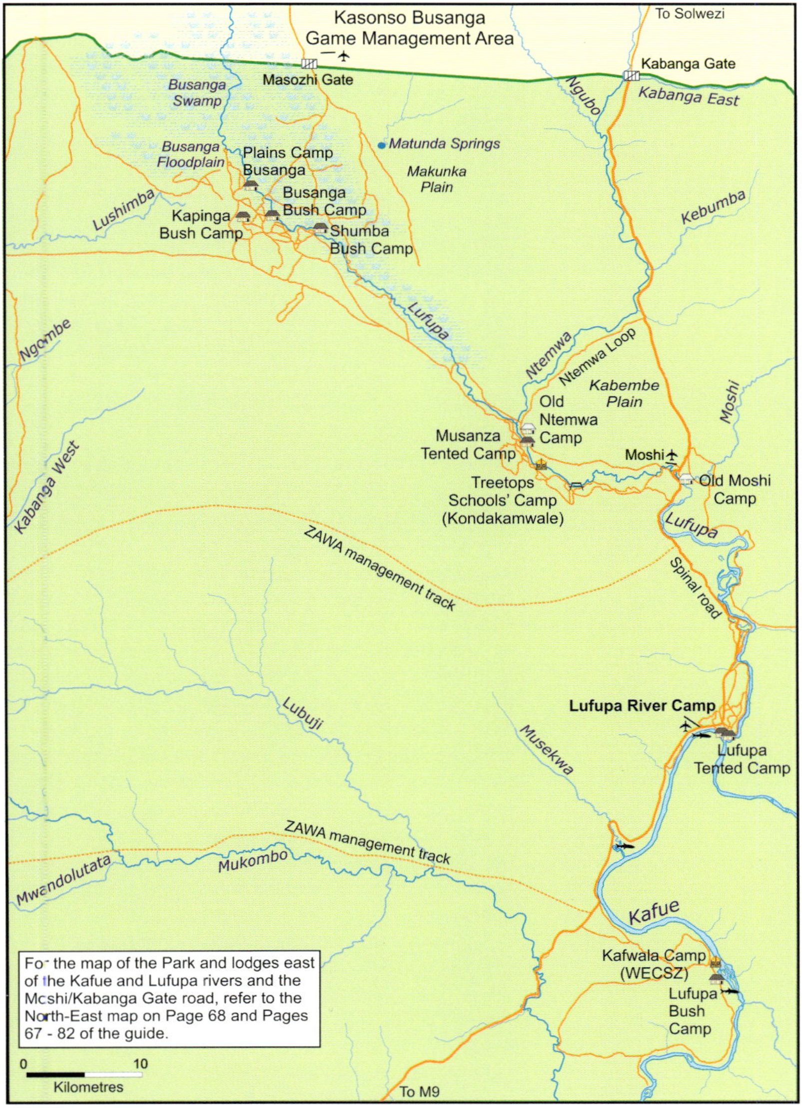

Roads and camps in the North-West Area.

1. The Southern part, which includes a stretch of the Kafue River with superb riparian woodland, islands and rapids of Kafwala - an outstanding place for birders and for otter watching - one of the original lodge sites and then northwards up to the confluence of the Kafue and Lufupa near Old Ntemwa, the site of another original KNP camp.

2. The Busanga Plain with five relatively new seasonal camps.

There is excellent wildlife viewing from all the camps throughout this area, and very good fishing along the Kafue and Lufupa Rivers. For self-drive campers there are *no campsites* available at present within the Park in the North-West area.

SOUTHERN PART OF THE NORTH-WEST AREA

Driving north from the M9 Highway Entrance Gate, after 32 km along the Spinal Road look out for the well sign-posted turning on the right at S14°46'109" E26°04'402", which goes to Kafwala, a great place for a break even if you are not staying there. You will have every chance of finding zebra, roan, hartebeest, sable, warthog, duiker, impala, puku, bushbuck, lion and elephant along the route. Rhino were often seen in the area between the Hook Bridge and Kafwala and this could be a good site for their eventual re-introduction. The scenery and fishing around Kafwala are outstanding, with overhanging riparian vegetation, palm trees, hippo-cropped riverbanks, deep pools, rocks and rapids. Further north the area around the Lufupa/Kafue confluence is one of the best places in the KNP for close-up views of hippo and crocodile, and the birders will enjoy opportunities for seeing specials such as Pel's fishing-owl, African finfoot, Chaplin's barbet and half-collared kingfisher.

In the northern part of this section follow the Spinal Road past Treetops Schools' Camp and Musanza Tented Camp up to the Busanga Plain. En route at old Moshi Camp, if you have enough time, turn off south-eastwards from Moshi loop where the track runs past pools with high banks on the lower Lufupa River (a good fishing spot for silver barbel) before eventually opening out beside small lateritic outcrops, onto the wide, nearly circular, Chibemba Plain. The centre of the plain is elevated by hot springs from which mineral salt precipitates have formed over thousands of years and which have led to the growth of a lush halophytic plant community. The salt mound is surrounded by hard clay nodules, worn smooth in places by the passing of animals, and the centre of the mound features hot saline pools. There is at least one active hot spring with a damp peat-like cone of organic material in a state of arrested or slow decomposition. Judging by the trails radiating from the mound to the surrounding woodlands and thickets, the area attracts many animals possibly from long distances. Herds of elephant, buffalo, zebra, eland, wildebeest, sable and roan are to be seen at the mound from time to time.

Leopards are often seen in the Lufupa area.

Lufupa Bush Camp: S14°48'113" E26°11'178"

Lufupa Bush Camp was originally part of the old Busanga Trails family, and was known as Kafwala Rapids Camp. Situated on the banks of the Kafue River and right on the Kafwala Rapids, an area of river known for its white water and birdlife, it has now been fully refurbished and has four ensuite chalets constructed from brick and thatch, each with a view of the rushing water of the rapids. Hammocks down by the edge of the river add to the relaxing feel of this little camp. The camp is lit with old-fashioned paraffin lamps and the meals are cooked outside over an open fire, often in front of the guests.

See *www. www.wilderness-safaris.com* for further information. For bookings contact *zambia@wilderness.co.zm* or phone +260.213.321-578.

Kafwala Camp: S14°47'853" E26°11'068"

The camp is situated just upstream from the Lufupa Bush Camp, facing a stretch of rapids, deep pools and tree-clad islands and is reserved for members of the Wildlife & Environmental Conservation Society of Zambia (WECSZ), although it is possible sometimes to stay there even if you are not a member, by arrangement with the WECSZ's National Office. There are two chalets, each with three single beds, and two with twin-beds. The toilets, shower and bathroom are separate. The camp is self-catering, but a deep freezer, fridges, lamps, crockery/cutlery, bedding and mosquito nets are available. There is also a dining room and lounge, a braai area, kitchen and pantry.

See *www.conservationzambia.com* for further information. For bookings contact WECSZ at *wecsz@zamnet.zm* or phone +260.211.251-630 or contact Terry Toms at *sunshineseedlings@gmail.com*

Lufupa River Camp: S14°36'996" E26°11'478"

This is one of the oldest camp sites in the Park but most of the original structures have been replaced by high-class *(c/d)* price modern buildings and large safari tents built on permanent stands. It is well situated along the main road to the Busanga Plain and, with the recently upgraded nearby airstrip and extensive network of wildlife viewing loops, it has rightly earned a high reputation as an outstandingly attractive and well-managed camp, with nine ensuite twin-bedded safari tents, including two extra-large tents with family rooms. There is a vibrant social club atmosphere here, which has become known as the *Kafue River Café* with a well-stocked bar and restaurant; a la carte meals and drinks are served during the day and early evening to resident guests.

See *www.wilderness-safaris.com* for further information. For bookings contact *zambia@wilderness.co.zm* or phone +260.213.321-578.

Lufupa Tented Camp: S14°36'941" E26°11'403"

This is a new *(d-e)* class luxury tented bush camp that is situated slightly downstream from the Lufupa River Camp on the Kafue River, with accommodation in nine ensuite, Meru-style tents built on permanent wooden decking, each with its own veranda and a wide view across the River. There is a central area situated on the riverbank for relaxation in style, complete with outstandingly comfortable safari camp furniture, a camp fire boma, dining area and small plunge pool. Like its sister camp, it is noted for its riverine scenery and wildlife viewing on the Riverside and Chibemba drives.

See *www.wilderness-safaris.com* for further information. For bookings contact *zambia@wilderness.co.zm* or phone +260.213.321-578.

Treetops Schools Camp: S14°24'232" E26°02'503"

A huge baobab tree is the central point at "Treetops" Conservation School Camp, known locally as "Kondakamwale" on the west bank of the Lufupa River near Moshi and old Ntemwa Camp. A few years ago the camp became very rundown, but recently it was renovated by the Treetops Society *(http://treetopskafue.webs.com/about.htm)* and is organised mainly for small groups of children from the schools in Lusaka in the dry season for short stays with the aim of educating the next generation about the country's wildlife. The camp has a boys' and girls' dormitory, three huts for teachers, a dining room, a classroom, ablution blocks with showers, and kitchen with freezers, all powered by solar panels.

Bookings are made through the Treetops Society. Contact Trish Anderson by phone +260.211.213-270 or Philip Bowen at *philipbowenisl@yahoo.co.uk*

Map of roads and camps of Busanga area.

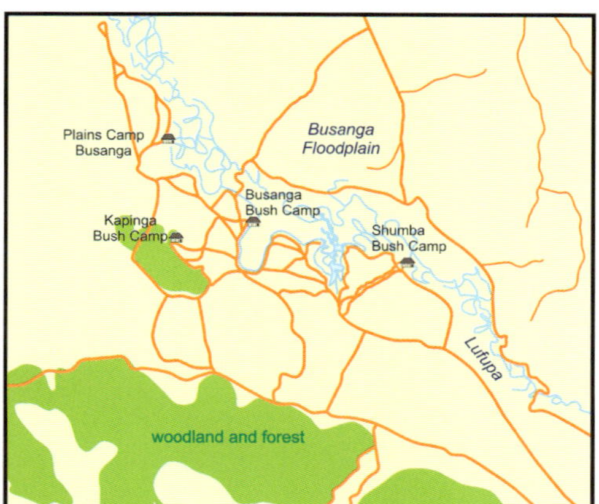

BUSANGA PLAIN

The 720 km² of the Busanga Plain is the only part of the Park where there are true swamps of any scale surrounded by wide grassy plains that together are thought to be part of a long-gone river system. Silken azure skies, early morning mists and breath-taking sunsets spread across the wide horizon of this huge grassy landscape. The plain is bisected by the Lufupa

River and provides rich grazing and water in the dry season for birds and many other animals, including herds of buffalo, wildebeest, zebra, roan antelope and puku. Large herds of red lechwe graze on the aquatic grasses in the meadows near the main Lufupa channel. The lechwe move northwards towards the swamp as the dry season progresses and as the middle Lufupa dries up. Sedges, rushes and reeds predominate in the swamp and it is here that you will be able to see sitatunga. Some of the wider channels are fished by village fishermen using traditional weir fishing techniques, usually between May and August and with spears in October and November.

Very little is known about the ecology of the Busanga. Nevertheless, there are plenty of opportunities to observe, study and photograph animals in this scenically outstanding setting. Lions are the most visible predator, but leopards, cheetahs, hyaenas and jackals are often seen. The bird life is superb, with excellent prospects to observe and photograph an astonishing celebration of most of Zambia's herons, egrets, pelicans, storks, ducks, geese, flamingos and cranes, and even the rare shoebill may be spotted if you are really lucky. According to geologists, Busanga was a huge lake in prehistoric times.

Musanza Tented Camp: S14°23'184" E26°02'054"

Situated on the southern fringe of the Busanga Plain beside the permanent pools of the Ntemwa River, Musanza is Wilderness Safaris rustic tented camp erected under thick shade in the riparian woodland, providing a wonderfully secluded and shady base for wildlife viewing in a diverse area. The "discoverer" tents are erected at the start of every safari season. Each has two proper beds with fine linen, a small hanging wardrobe and luggage rack. At the back of each tent is a private

WHAT TO SEE AND DO IN THE BUSANGA PLAIN						
Lodge/camp name	***Wildlife viewing***	***Boating***	***Fishing***	***Birding***	***Walking trails***	***Hot air Ballooning***
Musanza Tented Camp	+		+	+	+	
Shumba Bush Camp	+			+	+	+
Kapinga Bush Camp	+			+	+	+
Busanga Bush Camp:	+			+	+	+
Plains Camp, Busanga	+			+	+	

flushing toilet and a shower area. Hot water is brought to tents and poured into the bucket shower, which is then hoisted up into a tree with a pulley by the camp staff whenever a guest would like a shower. Lighting is provided by rechargeable lamps and traditional paraffin hurricane lanterns. The main area and dining room have views of the river, and as the dry season progresses, so the numbers and diversity of animals increases in the neighbourhood and viewing steadily improves.

> See *www.wilderness-safaris.com* for further information. For bookings contact *zambia@wilderness.co.zm* or phone +260.213.321-578.

Shumba Bush Camp:
S14°13'159" E25°52'350"

This *(e/f)* "Premier" class camp is situated in the centre of the Busanga Plain itself, built on raised wooden platforms with splendid views of the surrounding grassy plain. A maximum of twelve guests can be accommodated in outstandingly comfortable and spacious six twin-bedded, Meru-style tents with indoor and outdoor showers. Dining and bar area are

under a canopy of large fig trees. Dinners are served in a traditional style boma overlooking the Busanga Plain or indoors. Great emphasis has been placed by the management on the "guided" experience led by qualified, enthusiastic people with in-depth knowledge of the area and its wildlife. Guests will be flown by charter plane to Busanga airstrip near the Masozhi Entrance Gate and transferred from there to the camp by helicopter. Flying time to Busanga Airstrip at Masozhi is approximately 1hr 45mins from Livingstone and 1hr 20mins from Lusaka. Guests can also be driven to the camp depending on the time of the year, a trip of one to four hours with good wildlife viewing en route.

See *www.wilderness-safaris.com* for further information. For bookings contact *zambia@wilderness.co.zm* or phone +260.213.321-578.

Kapinga Bush Camp: S14°12'661" E25°48'976"

This is another of Wilderness Safaris "Premier" bush camps set on its own in Kalahari woodland on the southern edge of Busanga Plain. Kapinga Camp is designed to blend in with the environment, and natural products have been used as much as possible in the construction of the camp. There are four twin-bedded, ensuite, Meru-style tents with a private veranda in

front of each. Interiors are spacious and have all the modern conveniences. There is a dining room and bar area on raised decking with an adjacent plunge pool facing the Busanga Plain, set under a canopy of tall fig trees. Meals are served in the dining area overlooking the wilderness landscape. Qualified and knowledgeable guides lead all these drives. For those interested in birding, over 350 species have been recorded by visitors staying here, including Chaplin's barbet. Self-drive access is possible in 4x4 vehicles, but visitors are urged to plan carefully taking advice on the best route and state of the road from the Kafue Hook Bridge. Most guests at the camp fly in usually using the charter company recommended by Wilderness Safaris as for Shumba Camp.

> See *www.wilderness-safaris.com* for further information. For bookings contact *zambia@wilderness.co.zm* or phone +260.213.321-578.

Busanga Bush Camp:
S14°12'800" E25°51'184"

The last of the four Wilderness Safaris camps is located in the north-western part of the Busanga Plain and is about as wild as you can get in today's world, set in an unfenced mosaic of expansive grassy floodplains and water meadows that surround it. It caters for a maximum of eight guests in four well-appointed ensuite rooms built of shade-cloth and canvas with wall-to-wall views of the wildlife that frequents the plain in front of the camp. The dining and bar area are under a canopy of large fig trees. Dinners are served in a traditional style boma under the stars, overlooking the Busanga Plain, or indoors if you prefer. This camp nearly always provides exceptional opportunities for viewing lechwe, puku, roan, oribi, hartebeest, wildebeest, zebra and buffalo, with the wealth of wildlife on the Plain attracting leopard, wild dog, cheetah and several prides of lion. Access is as for Shumba and Kapinga.

See *www.wilderness-safaris.com* for further information. For bookings contact *zambia@wilderness.co.zm* or phone +260.213.321-578.

Plains Camp, Busanga:
S14°10'830" E25°49'165"

This is the most northern camp in the Park located on the Busanga Plain on an island site known as Two Fig Trees. It is operated by Mukambi Safari Lodge, the same company that owns the lodge near the Kafue Hook Bridge, described later in the section that covers the central part of the Park. The camp consists of four safari tents with twin or double beds, complete with the time-honoured open-air canvas bucket shower, basin and toilet. Dining room and bar are on a platform with great views over the plain. It is only accessible from July to the end of October and has been rated as one of Zambia's most remote and most attractive spots. It brings comfort to the wilderness; the guides are well-trained and experienced and all arrangements are professionally organized with knowledgeable and helpful staff.

See *www.mukambi.com* for further information. For bookings contact Edjan van der Heide at *info@mukambi.com* or *busangaplainscamp@gamail.com* or phone +260.97.613-5164.

The Lubalanzuki-Kaindabaila Hills.

CENTRAL AREA

The Central Area lies between Chunga, just south of the Kafue Hook Bridge, to the northern tip of Lake Itezhi-Tezhi. In addition to a major part of the KNP, this area also includes the Mumbwa Game Management Area (GMA) and the Namwala GMA to the east, and the Mufunta GMA to the west. There are three lodges on the east bank of the Kafue River, which are outside the Park and inside these GMAs, and are accessed by well-signposted signs on the left when coming from Lusaka and having passed through the Nalusanga Entrance Gate on the M9 Highway. *The first turning* that will take you to Puku Pan and Kaingu Lodges, is 217 km from Lusaka at S14°58'28" E26°27'08" and on to the D769, which is the gravel road that leads to Itezhi-Tezhi . The ZAWA Mweengwa check point at S15°16'53" E26°14'9[illegible]4" is 48 km down this road. After a further 3 km at S15°17'89" E26°14'17" turn right at the Kaingu Lodge and Puku Pan signs, and follow further signs to the two lodges. Both can also be accessed from the south through Itezhi-Tezhi on the D769. *The second turning* left into the GMA will take you to Mukambi Lodge and is well-signposted 9 km before the Kafue Hook Bridge at S14°57'584" E25°59'717".

Lwansanza River crossing on the Spinal Road in the Central area.

The Spinal Road to the south of the KNP from Chunga was under repair early in 2012 and might be open before the end of the year. There is rough bush track suitable only for 4x4 vehicles that follows the left bank of the Kafue River leading from Mukambi Lodge all the way down to Itezhi-Tezhi Town via Puku Pan and Kaingu.

To enter the KNP itself, take the second signposted turning to Chunga on the left 8 km after crossing the Hook Bridge at S14°56'683" E25°54'800". This will take you to three really worthwhile loop roads, namely Shishamba, Shishamba-Kafue and Chunga (also known as Mukambi), all of which are still being upgraded. Visitors are advised to check on the status of the roads and loops at the lodges and at the Area Warden's office at Chunga CAMU.

Much of the Central Area is miombo woodland (see Chapter 1) and visitors should encounter roan, sable, hartebeest, kudu, reedbuck, bushbuck, zebra, eland, buffalo, lion, leopard and cheetah. Puku, impala and duiker are common, particularly on the loop roads. This part of KNP is a great place for bird parties, typically containing up to twenty or more species, mainly of territorial insectivorous birds. The parties travel through the woodland, and membership changes as the route leaves and enters individual territories. A party is often first noticed where one of its more conspicuous members is seen or heard, usually led by species such as fork-tailed drongo or Arnot's chat. Joining these parties from time to time and also being observed on their own are the common scimitarbill, Africa hoopoe, barbets, honeyguides, woodpeckers, pipits, cuckoo shrikes, eremomelas, miombo barred warbler, hyliotas, flycatchers, chinspot batis, tits, spotted creeper, orioles, brubru, southern puffback, grey-headed bush shrike, fork-tailed drongo, violet backed starling, yellow-throated petronia, weavers, seed-eaters and cabanis's bunting. By any standards, this is an ornithologist's paradise. The seldom-used Western Boundary track also offers good prospects for the more adventurous birder after miombo species, but travelling along this track, where it forms the boundary with the Mufunta GMA south of the main M9 highway, requires careful planning - preferably with an experienced guide and with up to date information on the state of the track, especially whether it has been graded.

PLACES TO STAY IN THE CENTRAL AREA

Mukambi Safari Lodge
Heron Camp
Chunga Camp
Puku Pan Safari Lodge
Kaingu Safari Lodge
Kafumba Kwale Camp

Canoeing along the middle reaches of the Kafue River.

WHAT TO SEE AND DO IN THE CENTRAL AREA						
Lodge/camp name	***Wildlife viewing***	***Boating***	***Fishing***	***Birding***	***Walking trails***	***Cultural visit to local villages***
Mukambi Safari Lodge	+	+	+	+	+	
Heron Camp	+	+	+	+	+	
Chunga Camp	+		+	+		
Puku Pan Safari Lodge	+	+	+	+	+	+
Kaingu Safari Lodge	+	+*	+	+	+	+
Kafumba Kwale Camping Site	+		+	+		
† * Additional option is a 1-3 day canoeing safari						

Although rocks and rocky outcrops occur in several places throughout the Park and are great venues for the more adventurous, the most impressive of these are the Lubalanzuki and Kaindabaila cluster of dark granite rounded hills between Lake Itezhi-Tezhi and Chunga, and at the red granite ridges at Itezhi-Tezhi itself (in the Southern Area). These hills make attractive walks for the hiking enthusiast but they are difficult to reach at the moment. The rock hyrax, elephant and sable antelope are often observed here. Culturally they are of great significance to the Ba Ila people of Chief Kaingu who lived here at one time. It is said that Kaindabaila was used as an altar for sacrifices, and in times of drought, appeals for rain were made to the ancestral spirits from the top of the highest hill. There are magnificent views over the Kafue Valley from here that carry across the seemingly endless miombo woodlands that shimmer with the heat haze into the far horizon to the west.

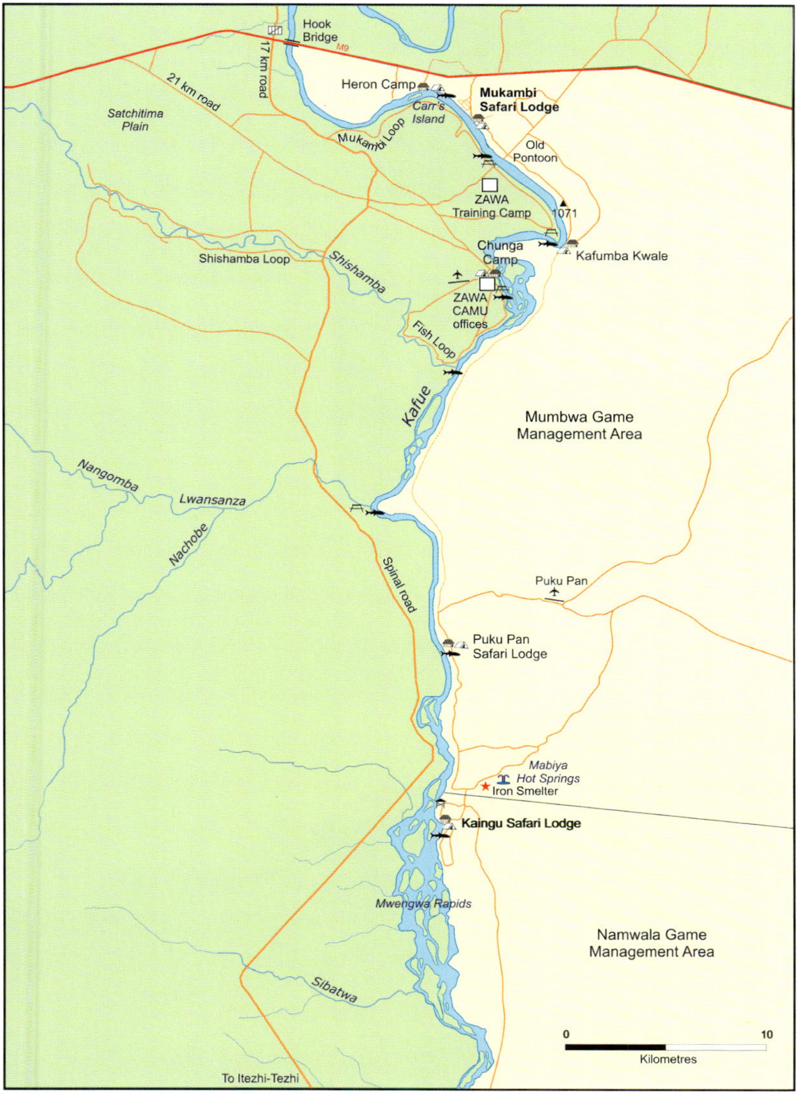

Roads and camps of the Central Area.

Mukambi Safari Lodge: S14°58'611" E25°59'532"

The outstandingly well-appointed year-round lodge is in class *(d)* and is situated within the Mumbwa Game Management Area set amongst mature woodland with some large shady trees lining a wide stretch of the Kafue River. Although located outside the Park, Mukambi has become a successful hub for the northern, central and southern Park areas and sets the pace for development of year-round tourism. There are eight ensuite, twin-bedded chalets, one family-sized, double bedroom chalet for four and one luxury riverside villa that has two ensuite bedrooms also for four and affords great privacy. Each unit has its own veranda facing the river. The dining room seats 24 with well-spaced tables on decking overlooking the river adjacent to the lounge. Together with the conference room there are three tiers of teak decking and there is a

separate bar, library and lounge between the main reception desk and dining room. A bonus, especially during the hot season, is the small swimming pool with adjacent shallow children's pool, well set up with sun loungers and umbrellas, a short stride from the dining room. There is also a camp fire/braai area close by on the riverbank shaded by Phoenix palm trees where weavers nest every year.

The serviced camping site is being relocated with new stands for four cars, each stand having a thatched roof to provide shade and some shelter from the rain. Showers with H&C water and flush toilets are provided. Four large, ensuite tents will be available nearby during the 2012 season but enquiries should be made about both the campsite and tents well in advance.

See *www.mukambi.com* for further information.
For bookings contact
Edjan van der Heide at *info@mukambi.com*
or phone +260.97.613-5164.

Heron Camp: S14°57'893" E25°58'424"

Just 2 km to the west of the turning to Mukambi on the M9 Highway and about 6 km from the Hook Bridge is the turning on the left to Heron Camp, which is also inside the Mumbwa GMA. It is situated about 2 km from the main road on an attractive site that slopes down steeply to the riverbank. A lodge is under reconstruction, but a campsite has been developed and already has five stands for self-catering visitors, H&C ablutions, toilets and braai facilities.

For bookings contact
Johan Wessels at
jm.wessels@hotmail.com
or phone
+260.97.577-0945.

Chunga Camp: S15°02'560" E26°00'003"

Chunga is an old camp in class *(a)* and although currently under renovation, it is possible to stay there either in a self-catering chalet or at the attached un-serviced camping site. The camp is attractively sited amongst big trees on the banks of the Kafue River. At present the camp is run by a resident caretaker on a self-catering basis with accommodation in four very basic, thatched, small rondavel-style chalets. There is a kitchen and raised unfurnished dining shelter that looks across the river and towards the floodplain to the west. External toilets, showers and a bath are shared by both. Firewood is not usually provided and visitors should bring bottled gas and water.

For bookings contact Esau Nebwe at
nexim@zamnet.zm

Kafumba Kwale : S15°02'254" E26°02'214"

This is a strictly seasonal camping site on the eastern banks of the Kafue River and inside the Mumbwa GMA that is reached by taking the riverside bush track south from Mukambi Safari Lodge. Kafumba Kwale is appropriately named, meaning the francolin's call, since this is a common sound heard in the surrounding bush, especially at dawn and dusk. The lodge is currently under renovation, but there is a usable camping site which is good place to stop for those undertaking the 4x4 route to the south.

For bookings contact
mutemwachambers@iconnect.zm

Puku Pan Safari Lodge:
S15°12'836" E25°58'675"

This well-sited *(c)* priced lodge on the Kafue River levee provides good opportunities for seeing wildlife around the woodland edge that fringes the small floodplains on the landward side, and in the miombo woodland that is interspersed by low granite outcrops. There are eight thatched cottages (including a larger family cottage) that blend in with the trees lining the riverbank. All of them have an ensuite bathroom with H&C water. The spacious rooms have local furniture and are decorated with ethnic fabrics. Every cottage has an individual veranda with fine views across the river. The lodge has a bar and dining room. Camping facilities with H&C showers are available nearby for a maximum of eight tents. For those who would prefer to fly in, there is a nearby airstrip S15°12'21" E26°02'51", 265 km from Lusaka and 295 km from Livingstone.

See
www.pukupansafarilodge.com
for further information.
For bookings contact
pukupan@zamnet.zm

Kaingu Safari Lodge: S15°17'817" E25°58'720"

This is a well-established, meticulously maintained, traditional-style lodge in the *(d-e)* price range. The lodge has four, large, twin-bedded, custom-made, Meru-style safari tents with raised wooden decks overlooking the river. All have bathrooms ensuite, each with its own alfresco stone shower facing the Kafue River, which you may choose to use in preference to the inside unit. One unit has an outdoor stone-clad bath. There is also a very comfortable family house that sleeps four, with two ensuite bedrooms, and with bunk beds provided for families with children. There is a bar, dining and lounge area, all on extensive wooden decking amongst tall trees on the riverbank – good for relaxation and bird watching. In addition, Kaingu has two riverside camping sites, each with its own private ablution facilities, one with two fully self-contained stands, and the other with

space for larger groups of 4x4 enthusiasts with shared ablutions. All have braai and washing-up facilities and meals can be arranged at the main lodge, that is about 200 metres away. A speciality for the fit and adventurous, which is operated from Kaingu Lodge, is the personally guided 1-3 day canoeing safari along the central Kafue River led by Bernard Calonne, incorporating guided walking and camping within the Park. There is always a haunting sensation that there have been very few who have tested the currents of this great river in this way before you, and that can be appealing or daunting, depending upon how you feel about travelling in a slim boat through uncharted territory. For those who would prefer to fly in, the Puku Pan airstrip is the nearest and easily accessible to Kaingu Lodge.

See *www.kaingu-lodge.com* for further information. For bookings contact *info@kaingu-lodge.com*
For bookings for canoe safaris contact Mawimbi Adventure Trails at *sikiliza@zol.co.zw*

"A paradise Livingstone never found" is what the brochure says and it is true that David Livingstone did not pass this way. Had he done so it is very probable that he might have likened the spot to a part of paradise on account of its isolated location deep in the bush amidst huge granite boulders, surrounded by mature riverine vegetation and overlooking a beautiful stretch of the Kafue River.

SOUTHERN AREA

The Southern Area embraces the whole of Lake Itezhi-Tezhi and the remainder of the Park to the west and south of the lake right down to KNP's southern-most point at Dundumwezi Gate, together with the GMAs of Nkala, Bilili Springs, Sichifulo and Mulobezi. For many years this part of the Park has been more or less cut off from the north, and the only way to travel between the two was on the poorly maintained D769 between Itezhi-Tezhi and the M9 through the Namwala and Mumbwa GMAs. When the long awaited improvement to the Spinal Road from Chunga to Ngoma via Lake Itezhi-Tezhi has been completed, the journey from north to south will be not only quicker, but much more interesting as the road follows the Kafue River the whole way and passes through varied habitats.

Lake Itezhi-Tezhi has become an important new feature of the KNP and an added attraction. Sunsets over the lake are a source of vivid memories of warm tropical evenings, fishermen returning in dugout canoes to their homes beyond the Park, silhouetted against the tranquil water and the sounds of nightjars and crickets as the night closes in. The dam was built to manage the flow of water to the Kafue Gorge hydro-electric station further downstream with the dam wall being made entirely from rocks without any concrete. After four years working night and day, it was completed at the end of 1977. The resulting lake covers 370 km^2 and has a level that fluctuates about 10 metres every year between the rains and the end of the dry season. A whole new range of habitats was created, the most obvious being the annually flooded grasslands on the lake edge. The exposed mud flats that have become grassed over, leaving residual shallow pools here and there, have become attractive breeding and feeding places for many birds, fish, amphibians and invertebrates – great for wildlife viewing throughout the year. The lake has also created many new opportunities for fishing and wildlife viewing and provides an environment in which the dynamic processes of colonization, development and growth

BUILDING THE DAM WALL

In his superb archaeological report on "Man on the Kafue" Dr Robin Derricourt poignantly described that there was a price to pay beyond the cost of the engineering works. He wrote: *Team members would return to the river in the evening, or sit near the base house watching the sun over the Kafue National Park where the sharp green line of woodland cut the incredible mixture of pink and blue, imaging a sheet of water over the area in view. The balance of nature, which suggested many millennia of hunting, food-gathering, fishing and farming can be destroyed in almost moments. We hope that some of our appreciation of the area we experienced for four months will live in our efforts to record permanently aspects of man's experience of it through his history of settlement there.*

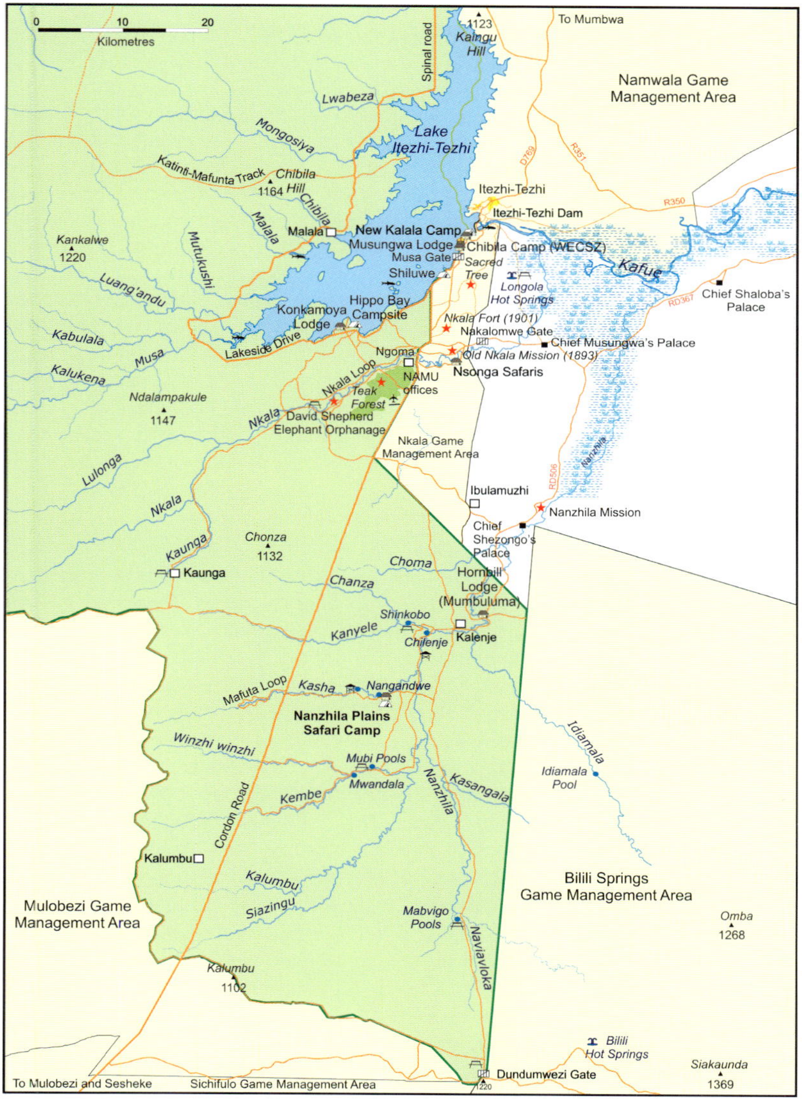

Roads and camps in the Southern Area.

ELEPHANT ORPHANAGE PROJECT

Game Rangers International (GRI) is supporting proactive species protection in the KNP through a special anti-poaching unit, ranger training and welfare support. Since early 2008 GRI with help from the David Shepherd Wildlife Foundation has established an Elephant Orphanage Project, to rescue, rehabilitate and release elephants orphaned as a direct result of poaching, back into the wild. See *www.gamerangersinternational.org* for further information. Visits from the public are welcomed. The Orphanage is situated 12 km south-west from Ngoma along the south Nkala Loop at S15°57'892" E25°51'931"

can follow paths of ecological succession. Furthermore, birdlife around the lake (90% of which lies within the Park boundary), has proliferated and fish breeding areas have become extended; hippo, crocodile, otters, herons and cormorants thrive. Unfortunately, disturbance by fishermen remains a constant threat. Local fishermen may take bigger catches than they did in the parent river, but disturbance on the islands accompanied by netting the inflow channels, tends to hinder tranquillity and holds back the natural system.

One of the more remarkable wildlife spectacles is the gathering of black barbel below the dam wall where, at times when water is released, large numbers of fish can be seen swimming strongly against the current in an endeavour to move upstream, their curved shapes and movements resembling salmon leaping on their return from the sea to breed in the upper reaches of rivers.

The sandstone hills that remain to the west of Lake Itezhi-Tezhi and on some of the large islands in the lake are of particular interest and worthy of being botanical special areas because of the deciduous miombo vegetation which grows in this habitat. Here you have a chance of seeing the heavily-built, dark-brown mottled savanna monitor lizard *Varanus albigularis* that has its evolutionary ancestors in the Miocene epoch some 69 million years ago, living now in Kafue amongst the rocks on the ridges near the Spinal Road to the north of the Musa River. The Shibatwa Hills beyond, in the central area are more or less inaccessible at the moment, but with expansion of tourism these surely will become a valuable attraction one day.

Visitors to the area around the lake are advised to check at their camps and also at the Entrance Gate (S15°47'800" E250°59'995") before driving off into the Park as signposts are few and far between once off the main roads onto the loops. Many of the loops are still under repair or are liable to change of route depending upon the rains and the lake's water level.

The Southern Area is much more than just the lake. Immediately to its south is the Old Namitwi Loop situated within the Nkala GMA, a fine wildlife viewing area with seasonal pools, good grazing and browse set amidst varied habitats, deciduous thickets and recovering teak forest following a line of low granite hills to the east. The early rainy season, after the hunting has closed, is a good time to visit, when visitors should see kudu, zebra, blue duiker, roan, buffalo, hartebeest and sable, with the crested guineafowl calling from the thickets. The best drives are around the lake and to the loops around Ngoma. There is good viewing once you have left the immediate vicinity of the sadly derelict Ngoma Lodge and travel along the south Nkala Loop towards the Elephant Orphanage Project where wildlife becomes more prolific and less disturbed. Wildebeest, waterbuck, roan, sable, reedbuck, oribi, and grysbok should be encountered, and recent sightings have included wild dog, lion, leopard and a family of cheetah.

South of Ngoma is a 24 km^2 teak forest, a particularly good example of teak forest that is found on Zambezi sand soils in the Southern and Western Provinces of Zambia. Most have suffered from heavy logging and uncontrolled burning. The timber is selectively logged, as it is durable and highly valued for flooring and furniture as well as for building, mining timber and fence pests.

There are two important cultural sites in the area. *The Old Nkala Mission* is just outside the KNP boundary 8 km from Ngoma on the road to Namwala at S15°54'324" E25°59' 944". The Mission itself became derelict long ago and only the foundations

PLACES TO STAY IN THE SOUTH

- New Kalala Camp
- Chibila Camp
- Musungwa Lodge
- Konkamoya Lodge
- Nanzhila Plains Safari Camp
- Hornbill Lodge - Mumbuluma

WHAT TO SEE AND DO IN THE SOUTHERN AREA						
Lodge/camp name	***Wildlife viewing***	***Boating***	***Fishing***	***Birding***	***Walking trails***	***Cultural visit to local villages***
New Kalala Camp	+	+	+	+	+	+
Chibila Camp	+			+		
Musungwa Lodge	+		+	+		
Konkamoya Lodge	+	+	+	+	+	+
Nanzhila Plains Safari Camp	+			+	+	+
Hornbill Lodge - Mumbuluma	+	+	+	+	+	

Nakalomwe Hill 8 km from Ngoma is the site of Old Nkala Fort, which has spectacular views over the Park and the Kafue Flats and can be reached via a well-established track.

remain, but it has its place in history as it was the site of the first European settlement north of the Zambezi River in the region of the Kafue River. It was founded by the Primitive Methodist Church and was occupied from 1893 until about 1930. The *Old Nkala Fort* is also about 8 km from Ngoma at S15°53'111" E25°59'147" and can be reached by driving along the road back towards Itezhi-Tezhi to S15°53'428" E25°58'204" where there is a signpost to Namwala on the right. After 1 km the road comes to the foot of Nakalomwe Hill where the overgrown track to the top of the hill remains marked by a stone verge, leading up to the low stone walls of the Fort. There is a superb view all round from the Fort that looks over the surrounding countryside, stretching far over the wide woodland horizon, to Lake Itezhi-Tezhi to the west and the Kafue Flats to the east. Originally built as a police fort in 1901 and manned by the Barotse Police, it was used later as the base for the first civil administration in the land of the Ba Ila and was finally abandoned in 1904. At one time it

was thought that the Cape to Cairo railway would pass through Nkala on its way from Livingstone to the emerging copper mines.

South from the Shakalongo Plain, the Winzhi-Winzhi, Kasha, Kanyele, Chilenje and Mubi Pool loops always provide interesting wildlife viewing since herds of buffalo (not common at the moment but historically very abundant), elephant, cheetah and prides of lion are sighted in these areas. There are several winter thorn trees along the Kanyele River and these are important in the nutrition of many species, particularly elephant, since the fruits (large pinkish curly pods) have a high protein content and both fruits and leaves are plentiful in late winter when most deciduous trees are shedding their leaves and when grasses are generally lying dormant and low in protein.

The Nanzhila Plains at the southern end of the Park are smaller and with more varied habitats than the Busanga Plain. These grasslands are also rich grazing grounds for all the species of antelope that you can find on the Busanga, except lechwe and surprisingly puku. This is an attractive landscape of open grasslands, mopane and large termitaria, interspersed by low woodland ridges, thickets and winding river channels that leave scattered pools and rich pastures in the watercourses and on the levees during the dry season.

The soils in the area are alluvial light to dark clays and their high nutrient level, annually enriched by flooding, together with an unusually large number of termite mounds covered in trees and shrubs (that have been referred to by scientists as "nutrient hotspots") enable the sector to support large numbers of grazers and grazer-browsers.

Top: Exotic crayfish (Cherax quadricarinatus) *found in the Kafue River below Itezhi-Tezhi Dam.*

Bottom: The spillway at Itezhi-Tezhi dam at full flow.

This part of the KNP is a superb place for bird watchers, and an undoubted attraction is the endemic black-cheeked lovebird, which breeds in and around the Nanzhila Plains and at one place outside of the Park along the Machili River south of Mulobezi. From July to August, the Nanzhila River also hosts Zambia's only regular breeding colony of about 100 pink-backed pelicans. Their surprisingly insubstantial stick platform nests are built in small *Acacia polyacantha* trees just 2-3m high. Other special birds to look out for near Nanzhila and at Mubi Pool 15 km to the south are Fülleborn's and rosy-breasted longclaws, wattled crane, saddle-billed stork, ground hornbill, woodland kingfisher, black crake, grey-headed parrot, black coucal, cisticolas (Luapula, chirping, trilling, tinkling, short-winged, pale-crowned, rattling and red-faced), neddicky, dark capped and yellow warblers, African pygmy goose, squacco and rufous-bellied herons, African and lesser jacanas, arrow-marked and Hartlaub's babblers, the little rush and lesser swamp warblers, mosque and red-breasted swallows and the five species of francolins/spurfowl namely red-necked, Swainson's, crested, Shelley's and Natal.

New Kalala Camp: S15°46'186" E26°00'862"

The Lodge was built in 1978 shortly after Itezhi-Tezhi dam was completed, to replace the original, highly popular, palm-clad Kalala Island Camp, which was engulfed beneath the waters of the dam. New Kalala nestles into the hillside and has marvellous views to the dam wall and across the lake to the north and west. It is organised around solid hexagonal brick chalets, a large, well-stocked indoor bar with constant TV, a swimming pool and an open dining room with a braai area that face the lake. There are seven ensuite, spacious

chalets with double and single beds and their own verandas, and two traditional, thatched rondavels with single beds. There are also two well-spaced camping sites close to the lodge but set apart from it, that can accommodate up to 25 vehicles. Each site has its own showers and toilets with H&C water. Firewood is provided free of charge. The lodge is probably one of the best places anywhere to view rock hyraxes that sport themselves amongst the large rocky outcrops on the hillside all around the lodge. New Kalala is class (c) and has developed a reputation as a hub and meeting point for trips to the southern part of the Park. A fishing competition full of bonhomie is held here every September that attracts fishermen with their motorboats from Lusaka, Livingstone, the Copperbelt and beyond.

See *www.newkalala.com* for further information. For bookings contact *info@newkalala.com* or phone +260.211.290-914, or +260.213.263-179.

Chibila Camp: S15°46'639" E26°00'406"

This quaint, self-catering camp (Chibila means rock hyrax in the Ila and Tonga languages) is set high above Lake Itezhi-Tezhi amongst large granite rocks and paperbark trees about 5 km from the Musa Entrance Gate further to the west on the D769 which leads into the Park. It blends into the natural environment with panoramic views over the lake, some of the best you can find to accompany a sundowner and braai. Accommodation comes in the form of double and family brick chalets with four single beds in each, all ensuite with toilet, hand-basin and H&C showers. Adjoining dining, lounge and braai area are set between huge red granite boulders. The camp is self-catering so it is essential to bring adequate food and drinks for your stay, although you can have meals at either New Kalala or Musungwa Lodge. The competent resident cook can prepare

food for you on request. There are also refrigeration facilities. The camp now also offers limited camping facilities, but you must be totally self-contained. It is mainly, but not exclusively, used by members of the Wildlife and Environment Conservation Society of Zambia (WECSZ).

See *www.conservationzambia.com* for further information. For bookings contact WECSZ at *wecsz@zamnet.zm* or phone +260.211.251-630

Musungwa Lodge: S15°47'00" E26°00'19"

Musungwa is a large property perched on the top of a granite ridge and was the first lodge to be built just outside the Park on the southern shore of Lake Itezhi-Tezhi just after the dam was completed. Built as a recreational and conference centre, it has suffered through poor road infrastructure, especially the almost total lack of maintenance over many years of the D769 access road leading to it from the M9 Highway. However, for large groups looking for a convenient class *(b-c)* base from which to explore the lakeshore and to strike deep into the southern part of the Park, it is well-positioned and reasonably priced. The lodge has 11 brick-built rectangular twin-bedded and 14 four-bed chalets (all ensuite) set in a line along the ridge, and a large family house that sleeps up to 12. There is a dining room and a well-stocked bar and comfortable seating with outside tables set on a terrace facing the lake, and a large swimming pool, tennis courts, squash court and sauna.

See *www.musungwalodge.co.za* for further information. For bookings contact *zamker@zamnet.zm* or phone +260.211.273-493.

Konkamoya Lodge: S15°52'054" E25°52'980"

Situated on a promontory on the south-western shore of Lake Itezhi-Tezhi, Konkamoya Lodge, previously known as Cooke's Camp, is in the price range *(e)*, and is reached by following the rough lakeside track known as Lakeside Drive, that leads off the main road from Itezhi-Tezhi to Ngoma, skirting closely round the edge of the lake where it is constructed right on the lakeshore. The turning at S15°52'820" E25°52'547" has a sign at the junction of the tracks to the lodge and its satellite camping site S15°52'540" E25°53'065", which is marked as Hippo Bay Camp. The lodge has five twin-bedded, large luxury tents ensuite with H&C showers set discretely in line facing the lake in the fairly dense cover of lakeside riparian vegetation and overlooking a wide expanse of open grassland. There is a raised bar and dining room with fine views across the lake. The nearby Hippo Bay camping site has facilities for six cars and includes a simple rustic ablution block with H&C showers and basins, flush toilets and washing up facilities. Water is pumped from a borehole and is safe to drink from the taps.

See *www.konkamoya.com* for further information. For lodge bookings contact *info@konkamoya.com* and for camping contact Chris Cooke at *bwanasafari@gmail.com* or phone +260.97.737-6797

Nanzhila Plains Safari Camp: S16°16'465" E25°55'510"

It takes about two hours to reach the lodge from Dundumwezi Gate following the all-weather Cordon Road route (87 km), and approximately an hour and a half taking the Plains Road to the east, that is only passable in the dry season. The ZAWA staff at the Gate should be consulted about the state of the Plains Road. The lodge has three large, ensuite safari tents on teak platforms, each with its own veranda and three ensuite chalets. There is a large thatched dining room with bar and barbecue area set beneath an enormous jackal berry tree. The camping site has four stands able to handle a total of 24 campers at any one time and has toilets and H&C showers all in traditional bush-camp style and serviced by the main camp. The chalets and tents are placed on either side of a large, heavily thatched, central dining room and bar built on a raised platform overlooking Nangandwe Pool where jacanas skip over the water lilies and where herds of waterbuck, impala and elephant are frequent visitors. All the buildings meld unobtrusively into the natural environment adjacent to the elephant path that meanders through the site, much older than the lodge itself. This continues to be used by bull elephants that sometimes walk purposefully through the lodge to the lower Nanzhila River. The bird hide set beside a permanent pool at S16°14'252" E25°57'686" is a short drive from lodge and is a good place for seeing flocks of black-cheeked lovebirds.

See *www.nanzhila.com* for further information. For bookings contact *info@nanzhila.com* or telephone Steve Smith on +267.72.123-002

Hornbill Lodge - Mumbuluma: S16°11'925" E26°01'891"

This is a private lodge, which takes its name from the Mumbuluma Concession in the KNP managed by Hornbill Safaris. It is well-spaced in riverine woodland beside the lower Nanzhila River, and anyone wishing to stay there must do this by prior reservation with the owners; there are no booking agents. The lodge will only accept one booking at a time with a maximum of eight people. It has four twin-bedded, brick-built chalets, a bar and dining room, and a boat jetty.

See *www.mumbuluma.com*
for further information.
For bookings contact Sergio Segura at
hornbillspain@terra.es

Below: The lower Nanzhila River before it enters the Kafue Flats floodplain.

B 182 ANI

MANAGING THE KAFUE NATIONAL PARK

A primary objective of all recognised National Parks is their role in conserving regional biological diversity. Biodiversity (as it is better known) is one of the key terms in conservation, encompassing the richness of life and the diverse patterns it forms. The Convention on Biological Diversity (CBD) defines it as "the variability among living organisms from all sources including terrestrial, marine and other aquatic ecosystems and the ecological complexes of which they are part". This includes the diversity *within* species, *between* species and the diversity of ecosystems. Human society depends on this extraordinary diversity for its incalculably important role in maintaining ecosystem services to support human well-being and life on earth. These essential services include the maintenance of soil fertility and the enhancement of soil formation and erosion mitigation, cleansing of the atmosphere, climate regulation and carbon sequestration, pollination services, and most importantly maintaining water cycles and providing clean water to adjacent areas.

Equally important is the enormous potential that exists in the world's biodiversity for future medicines and food plants. Medicines originating from wild species have already saved millions of lives, with 40% of all medical prescriptions originating from plants and animals. There are 80,000 species of edible plants known on Earth, but 90% of the world's food comes from a mere 20 of these species. Edible plant species, both those we know of and those we don't, offer a tremendous resource of

Above: The fruit of the sausage tree is widely used in traditional medicine for skin disorders.

Left: One of the challenges facing management in the KNP is to develop roads for year-round access.

Keeping pristine wilderness areas intact is a priority for management of parts of the KNP.

possibilities that could greatly add to the security of our food. Breeding cultivars with their wild counterparts can also confer resistance to diseases and increase crop yield. There is no doubt that the KNP and the adjacent GMAs host a treasure trove of plants and animals that are already making a significant contribution to Zambia's ecological stability, and that there are species within these areas that could be of considerable economic value in the future.

Although the economic and ecological arguments for conserving biodiversity are very powerful, we should never forget moral, ethical, and philosophical considerations, as many people think it is wrong to let species go extinct and to treat nature as if it has been designed for our convenience and abuse. The extraordinary celebration of biodiversity that the KNP has on show inspires and enriches our lives, and these aesthetic, spiritual and cultural "services" are in themselves strong motivations to keep the Park intact for the benefit of future generations.

WHY MANAGEMENT IS NECESSARY

Whilst efforts are made to keep the KNP as a natural area and stop the loss of species, the mere action of demarcating the boundary introduces an element of artificiality. Similarly, other man-made features, such as roads, buildings, signposts, firebreaks, power lines and the Itezhi-Tezhi Dam, are unnatural yet unavoidable features. The Park is a special place established for man by man and is kept in as undisturbed a state as possible, allowing natural succession to proceed, and preserving biodiversity whilst at the same time providing the means for our enjoyment. The Park managers face daily pressures caused by changes both within and outside the KNP, particularly the effects of a fast growing human population, now at about 13 million - over three times higher than it was at the time independence was gained in 1964. Despite these difficulties, ZAWA has done well over the years to ensure that none of the Park boundary has been encroached, and there are encouraging cases of how species can respond to protection from poaching, such as the story of the Busanga red lechwe. At about the time the Park was being formed in 1948 their total number was exactly 71. By 1971 this had increased to 1,163 and in 2011, after removal of man the predator, there were more than 6,000.

Experience in other Parks has shown that the change from unspoilt wilderness to crowds of cars and people can happen all too quickly. Too many elephants concentrating in small areas can result in significant habitat transformation and loss of woody vegetation, and uncontrolled fires can bring about simplification of plant communities and the loss of biodiversity. To avoid additional problems, such as water pollution, soil erosion,

With the ever increasing demand for tourism facilities, every effort is made to keep the footprint of camps to a minimum.

Elephants can reach browse inaccessible to all other terrestrial mammals in the KNP.

population imbalances caused by poaching or widespread disease, the KNP is managed on scientific principles, involving research and a realistic view of how to carry out management. The whole situation is a bit circular: the more we strive to provide facilities for human enjoyment, the more scientific management is needed; the more one tries to maintain the integrity of the environment, the greater the need to control and the less natural the system. If this is understood and accepted, then use and abuse need not be synonymous so the mistakes made of overcrowding and unnatural disturbance in parks in other parts of world could be avoided here. The real art is how to maintain wilderness values at the same time as providing for management, amenities and comfort for people.

Most of these principles have not changed much over the years and as long ago as 1961 Professor Boughey, the eminent ecologist, wrote this after he visited the Park:

"Kafue National Park provides a unique opportunity, not only for the preservation of many types of animal and plant life otherwise now threatened with imminent extinction, but also for the investigation of many ecological problems, a fundamental knowledge of which will not only advance learning as such, but will be applicable to management practices for the economic development of the country as a whole".

Visitors to the KNP will soon notice that there are often several species of mammals living together and occupying more or less the same area. Through the processes of evolution and adaptation in the savanna ecosystems of Africa, these areas have the highest animal biomass of anywhere on earth. How this is achieved is associated with the phenomenon of "ecological separation" whereby each species along the food chain of predator and prey, herbivore and carnivore, occupies and feeds within its own niche, which is uniquely separated in space and composition from the next.

There are few places where this ecological manifestation is better observed than in Kafue where many different species of large animals feed at different levels and on different plants in a harmonious relationship with each other. Elephant feed in the high canopy of trees, which is a vegetation level often shared with giraffe (probably an empty niche in Kafue), and being browsers and grazers they feed at all levels from the tops of trees down to the grass, leaves, and fruits on the ground, and in some instances even on roots and tubers below the surface of the soil; at an intermediate level large antelope like eland and kudu are mostly browsers but do graze, whilst hartebeest, sable, roan and waterbuck are mostly grazers; at the lower levels, often just browsing in thickets or predominantly grazing in the plains and dambos where there are several species, such as duiker, bushbuck, impala, puku and lechwe; and then there are the really heavy grazers such as elephant, buffalo, zebra and wildebeest. All these animals share the same ranges, living harmoniously in different niches within the ecosystem. It is not unusual to see 20 or more species of large mammals in a day's travel.

To add to the spectrum and to the animal biomass, you will find warthog, bushpig, hippo and carnivores such as lion, leopard, wild dog and otters, water monitors, monkeys and baboons. The

A warthog kneels to graze and to dig out roots and bulbs.

KNP MANAGEMENT BLOCKS

1. *Nalusanga the North-East (Block1): east of the Hook Bridge and south of the Kafue River eastwards to the Mumbwa District boundary and south along the north side of the Mumbwa-Kaoma section of M9 main road.*
2. *Lunga-Busanga: the North-West (Block 2a) lying north of the Kafue River and east of the Lunga.*
3. *Lufupa-Busanga: the North-West (Block 2b) lying to the west of the Lunga River and across Busanga Plain to the Western Boundary.*
4. *Chunga North-West (Block 2c): astride the M9 main road south of the Mukombo River and north of the Nangomba/Lwansanza west to the Western Boundary.*
5. *Central (Block 3): south of the Nangomba/ Lwansanza River to the Musa River and west of Lake Itezhi-Tezhi to the Western Boundary.*
6. *Nkala or South (Block 4a): south of the Musa River, east of Lake Itezhi-Tezhi to the north Nkala River and westwards to the Western Boundary.*
7. *Nanzhila or South (Block 4b): south of the Nkala River to Dundumwezi.*

aquatic environment that provides the water of life to all the species is shared by crocodiles, hippo, turtles and fish. Among the primates there is an interesting interface between the yellow baboon *Papio cynocephalus,* which is widely distributed, and the larger and darker coloured chacma baboon *Papio hamadryas* that is recorded in the southern part of the Park only. You will be able to see the vervet monkey *Cercopithecus pygerythrus*, the bushbaby *Otolemur crassicaudatus* and night ape *Galago moholi* in most places.

MANAGEMENT ZONES OF THE KNP

The Zambia Wildlife Authority (ZAWA) is responsible for the entire national protected area system, nearly a third of the country, vested in them by the Zambia Wildlife Act of Parliament No 12 of 1998. Through this Act and the National Policy for National Parks and Wildlife, ZAWA is responsible for management, control and regulation of 19 National Parks and 36 Game Management Areas. This is an onerous task that deserves the support of everyone, and after your journey in KNP you will be able to appreciate the vast area and huge range of activities that have to receive attention.

Day-to-day administration of the Park is in the hands of the Western Regional Manager, who also manages the Park's Business Centre at an office in Mumbwa Town at S14°590'491" E27°03'902", turning right onto a gravel side-road at the first roundabout. Conservation, development, research and management are all carried out in the Park itself by two Wardens, two Area Managers and by Wildlife Police Officers. There are also Ecologists responsible for research and management. The Warden's and Ecologists' offices are at Ngoma and Chunga catering for the south and north. If you have any questions regarding the management of the Park or its flora and fauna, don't hesitate to ask members of the Park staff.

The Park has always been divided for management into two sectors: the north and the south, and whilst that practice still continues, from the landscape point of view and to be able to appreciate ecological differences, it has been separated recently into seven blocks (see box for approximate descriptions). These are now being used to describe various kinds of concession that are offered to anyone who would like to invest in working with ZAWA and local communities on managing parts of the Park. This detailed information is included as it can help you appreciate how the Park is being developed, and it is also useful for managers and prospective investors. This is a busy time as the Park is being rapidly transformed and is becoming a Business Centre in its own right so that it can eventually become self-supporting. Until recently all development of lodges was managed by the ZAWA sector headquarters at Ngoma and Chunga where Wardens and Rangers-in-charge are based, leaving the central portion relatively undeveloped. Today much more emphasis is being placed upon developments around the edge of the Park where the communities reside. More information on these subjects can be obtained from ZAWA.

Above: KNP and the adjacent GMAs present some superb opportunities for investment in new camps and lodges.

KNP is surrounded by nine Game Management Areas that together cover an area of 45,406 km^2, adding a considerable area of land within which wildlife is conserved albeit less intensively and mainly for regulated hunting. At the same time photo-tourism is growing fast as seen in the 13 safari lodges and camps that are operating close to the Park. ZAWA looks after the management and conservation of all natural resources in them and should be contacted for more up to date information on the state of the roads and wildlife.

Below: Uncontrolled fires in the KNP significantly impact on many species of plants and animals.

Aside from poaching, uncontrolled bush fires are the biggest management problem as they affect most of the Park every year, sometimes burning thousands of hectares in a single conflagration.

Fire and firebreaks

Fires are mentioned throughout this book because they are so important in the ecology and long-term future of the Park. Uncontrolled burning is a nationwide phenomenon from which KNP is never spared and from June to October fires are often burning or have burnt large tracts of woodland and grassland, leaving the landscape looking devastated with burnt trees and grass turned to ash and dust everywhere.

There are many causes of uncontrolled bush fires and the subject is one that always generates a lot of debate, not least because it is against the law to cause a fire in a National Park. The main causes are firstly a forestry policy that goes back to early colonial days when it was generally accepted that if the bush, which refers to all woodland, forest, scrub and grassland, is going to burn, then burning it early in the dry season (called "early burning") is better for the environment than burning it late when fires are hot and can be very damaging. Other common causes are simply clearing the bush so that people can see and move around more easily; fires set by hunters to attract animals to the green flush that often but not always a follows a burn; village agriculturists and honey gatherers allowing fire to get out of control and passers-by who irresponsibly burn the bush for no reason at all.

In 1960 the celebrated ecologist Frank Fraser Darling, wrote that "*...in the course of the past thousand years in Africa the effect of man-made fire has shifted large areas of plant formations to a state [miombo] now taken for granted,*" and that early burning is unnatural and is "*a tool of despair.*" He went on: "*One of the most destructive effects of frequent burning, which can scarcely be detected* *annually and which needs a lively observation and capacity to remember, is the reduction in variety of plants present in the vegetation. Legumes are quickly lost and the larger-leaved herbs; then one or two species of grass, usually less palatable ones, become dominant in the sward. A vegetation of much reduced variety is inelastic in response to change or catastrophe... It should be considered as axiomatic that the practice of burning shifts the vegetational complex towards the arid or xeric; it is a continuous process of dehydration.*"

Many species, such as hartebeest, impala, roan, sable and wildebeest drop their young in the period August to November and, since this is the time of most stress for mothers and their calves, logically it should be the time of most tranquillity and security of food and cover - not maximum disturbance by burning of their habitats. In fire management there is not much doubt that burning the bush reduces plant biomass and holds back growth and regeneration. The problem is that burning does not just occur in the early dry season, but whenever there is anything to burn it gets burnt, whether in the early, mid or late season every year.

Quite apart from the immediate loss through burning at any time of leaves and grass, thereby inhibiting growth, fire has a bad effect on soils (removal of organic matter), disrupts nutrient cycles and causes damage to habitats of small mammals, birds and invertebrates. This virtual annual sterilisation process is detrimental in the long-term through converting much of the annual growth of grass and leaves into dust and ash every year. Widespread annual uncontrolled bush fires are evidently damaging many of the vegetation types, especially mopane, teak, riparian woodland and

Wildebeest feeding on fresh green growth that often but not always springs up after a bush fire. Animals are well adapted to this phenomenon, which often attracts antelope when the other vegetation is dry and less palatable.

ZAWA Wildlife Police Officers attending a patrol briefing session at Chunga Area Management Unit.

miombo - the latter over large tracts where the canopy is thinned, growth retarded and biodiversity diminished.

Until there are sufficiently large numbers of heavy grazers and browsers that will trample and consume grasses and combustible litter that will reduce the fire hazard, then about the only option is for society to stop random burning and to allow range managers, agriculturists, foresters and rural communities to follow the ZAWA policy of controlled early burning, thereby getting closer to a natural order in which natural succession can occur and allow a mosaic of different age classes of vegetation to become established. Management of bush fires over such a vast area is a daunting task that requires clear objectives, such as early burning firebreaks to prevent incursions into sensitive habitats, backed by adequate manpower, equipment and finance. When a more natural fire interval between burns becomes established, animal numbers will greatly increase and the land will be much more productive.

Where fire occurs every year in miombo woodland, there is little or no understorey, ground cover is thin and simplification of the plant and animal communities is always apparent. Fire degraded woodlands are recognised by the abundance of *Diplorhynchus, Uapaca, Terminalia* and *Combretum* species, stunted growth, sparse canopy and wide spaces between the remaining large trees. There are two features, which should be considered when thinking about miombo woodland as a habitat for large mammals and birds. Firstly, good quality miombo woodlands have a uniform open canopy at about 5-8 metres above the ground. Since giraffe are absent and the elephant population is relatively low, this canopy is a vast, unattainable and, therefore unused layer of browse vegetation. Secondly, where one or two very hot late fires have been followed by two or three years with early burning, the patches of burnt out woodland, are often re-invaded by miombo species, seen as low leafy shrublands or "Munga" as they are called. These areas provide a lot of browse for herbivores and attract elephant, eland, sable, hartebeest and kudu. To increase diversity and productivity in both species and in structure, a mosaic of young growth to mature canopy woodland, resembling a natural order, can be attained by fire management that eliminates uncontrolled annual burning.

Above: Waterbuck research in the Ngoma area.

RESEARCH AND MONITORING

To manage a Park with the diversity and complexity of a vast area like the KNP, focussed research and monitoring studies are an essential pre-requisite in order to provide ecological information and advice to ZAWA on all aspects of biodiversity conservation on the Park and adjacent GMAs. The following eight research and monitoring topics have been identified as priorities for management needs.

(i) Habitat management. Priorities include the status of critical habitats such as the Busanga Plain and swamps, the teak forests and mopane woodlands and riparian vegetation types.

(ii) Fauna. Field studies should focus initially on the status of threatened and flagship species, particularly those with restricted habitats, such as klipspringer, sitatunga, yellow-backed and blue duiker, and then eland, sable, roan, red lechwe, buffalo, cheetah, wild dog, leopard, lion and elephant. In addition, field studies will be required on the status of key birds, fish, reptiles, amphibians and invertebrates that must be prioritised for management planning and for establishment of special conservation measures if deemed necessary.

Below: Far too little is known about the distribution and status of most of KNP's reptiles such as the savanna monitor.

(iii) Physical factors. Soil, climate and water relations, especially evidence of erosion or changes in their ecological relationships must be monitored and included in Annual Work Plans.

(iv) Socio-economic factors. Socio-economic studies will need to be

Opposite: The KNP is an integral part of the 440,000 km² five-nations Kavango-Zambezi Transfrontier Conservation Area.

carried out by ZAWA working in close collaboration with NGOs and other stakeholders who will be involved in Community Based Natural Resource Management (CBNRM) activities and community development in the GMAs.

(v) Control and management of fire. The need for this has already been highlighted. In addition to planning and positioning fire-breaks, the implementation of monitoring and GIS mapping data and time-bound fire record keeping is essential.

(vi) Management and ecological impact of traditional fishing inside the Park and along the Kafue River. This topic will require in-depth study to examine usufruct rights and their ecological and social impacts in the Busanga/Kasempa, Kaingu/Kafue River and Nanzhila/Namwala fisheries.

(vii) Re-establish the laboratory and herbarium at Ngoma. A herbarium should be re-established either at Ngoma or a new one created at Chunga so that a study collection can be maintained for use by the Ecologists and visiting research workers.

(viii) Establish a linked integrated database and strengthen data storage and retrieval systems. There are several useful databases that are used by ZAWA, but these should be linked within a meta-database structure that can be integrated with a central database at ZAWA HQ. The KNP research team could also provide assistance in preparing interpretative material eventually for the Park's Visitor's Centre and for use by tourists and other researchers.

OPPORTUNITIES FOR TRANSFRONTIER CONSERVATION

KNP has recently become a significant part of the five-country Kavango-Zambezi Transfrontier Conservation Area known as the KAZA-TFCA. Embracing parts of Angola, Namibia, Botswana, Zimbabwe and Zambia, it is the world's largest transfrontier conservation area spanning over 444,000 km² – almost the size of Sweden. On 18 August 2011 the KAZA Heads of States signed the KAZA Treaty in Luanda, Angola, formally establishing a complex of areas into one entity that includes National Parks, Game Reserves, Forest Reserves, Conservancies, Game/Wildlife Management Areas and Communal Lands. The natural resources contained in the KAZA TFCA are critical to the sustainable development of the region on account of their inherent and enormous socio-

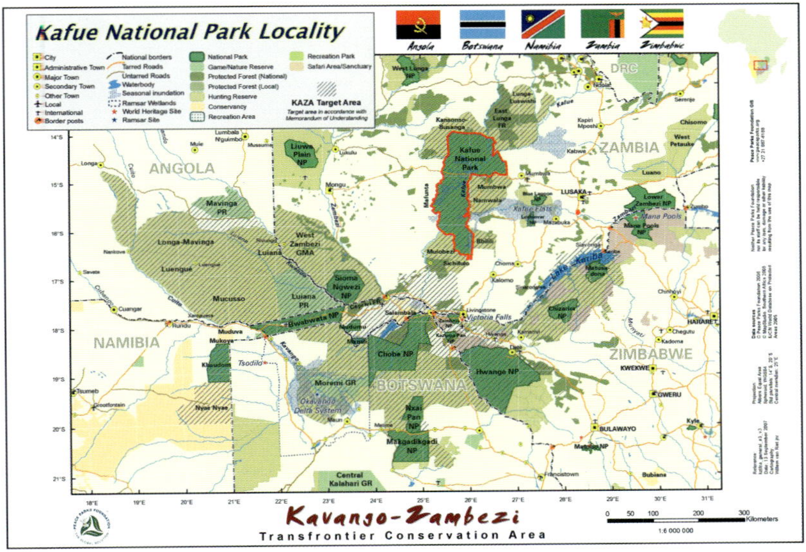

economic value. Furthermore, the biodiversity in the TFCA has the potential to insulate the region from the effects of climate change.

The KAZA-TFCA partner countries have identified tourism as one of the key drivers for socio-economic development of the region due to its strong multiplier effects, and they are determined to accelerate the growth of the tourism industry in the region within the context of sustainable development. All five governments have emphasised that socio-economic development in the region must benefit the local communities that live within and around the TFCA. These communities are the custodians of the resource and bear huge opportunity costs associated with biodiversity conservation, such as Human Wildlife Conflicts, which have contributed to household food insecurity. During the launch of the KAZA TFCA, the partner countries reaffirmed their commitment to regional economic integration through sustainable management of transboundary natural resources and tourism development.

The establishment of the KAZA TFCA is in line with the objectives of the Southern African Development Community (SADC) of regional economic integration and specifically the Protocol on Wildlife Conservation and Law Enforcement of 1999, which commits SADC Member States to "promote the conservation of shared wildlife resources through the establishment of transfrontier conservation areas". This is an exciting new development, which should help to boost tourism in Zambia in general and in the KNP in particular.

TRAVEL TIPS

VISAS AND ENTRY PERMITS

All visitors to Zambia should always check with the nearest Zambian immigration office on the latest visa requirements when planning their trip, as the rules change from time to time, as do the visa costs. If you are self-driving then it is essential that you make sure that all car documents are up to date and that you have US dollars (preferably) to pay for your car's temporary import permit (TIP), carbon tax, Third Party Insurance and Community Tax. A valid passport is required for entry into Zambia and Visa fees at the time of going to press are as follows:

- UK passport holder: $50 single entry and $80 double entry valid for 3 months
- US passport holder: same fees but valid for 3 years.
- All other visitors the same fees excluding SADC citizens who enter at no charge.

Nationals of all Commonwealth countries do not require visas to enter Zambia, except for the following countries:

Australia	New Zealand
Britain	Nigeria
Canada	Sri Lanka
Gambia	Sierra Leone
Ghana	Pakistan
India	Papua New Guinea

Multiple entry visas are not available at the border post, and are only available by application to embassies or to the Department of Immigration in Lusaka.

ZAWA Northern Area Management Unit office at Chunga - CAMU.

KNP rules and regulations

There is nothing worse than going on holiday to be met by a long list of rules and regulations, but some of these have to be called to the attention of all visitors to the KNP for their own safety, for the safety and security of the Park's fauna, flora and natural environment, and for the benefit and enjoyment of other visitors. All the Rules and Regulations for the Park are taken from the Wildlife Act and from the Zambian National Parks and Wildlife Policy. Always take advice from ZAWA staff or lodge staff if you are unsure of your route or what you are likely to see or be able to do. Enjoy your

- The Park opens at 06h00 and closes at 18h00, around sunrise and sunset, and you are expected to be in your lodge or camp before dark.
- Keep to the speed limits: 40 km/h on roads and 25 km/h on wildlife viewing loops.
- Animals have right of way: don't disturb them by sounding your horn or shouting.
- Do not leave your car as this can be dangerous; walking is only permitted with a licensed escort or guide.
- You can get out of your car however at designated fishing and picnic spots, but look around for dangerous animals before you do so.
- Never swim in any of the rivers or pools. Crocodiles are everywhere and usually hard to see even in shallow water, and there is always the risk of bilharzia.
- Do not play football, volleyball or cricket etc., and avoid making noise with your radio or music player.
- Take your garbage with you when you leave the Park.
- Do not throw lighted cigarettes out of the window as they can start bush fires.
- Don't collect plants, animals, flowers, stones or bits of wood as these all belong to the natural environment of the Kafue National Park.

visit, but please respect the environment and always have regard for other visitors. For everyone there are just a few important rules to remember as summarised in the box on page 133.

HEALTH AND SAFETY

Compared with travelling in remote deserts or high-risk mountainous country, personal safety in KNP is not something that should worry you too much as you are seldom far from water and the landscape is not very steep or particularly rugged. On the other hand, never forgot that this is wild Africa in which there are few rescue services or easily contactable medical facilities. It is important, therefore, to drive carefully, follow the Park rules and watch out for hazards such as deep potholes, hidden rocks, deep sandy ruts, fallen trees and animals that might cross unexpectedly in front of your car. Be particularly cautious when there is tall grass at the side of the road because it is often hard to know what this is concealing. These risks simply require careful driving and being alert to the state of your road and the land to either side.

There are some health and safety matters that you should be aware of and over which you should take normal precautions. Always bring along a small first aid kit. Apart from basic first aid kits at all lodges and camps, the only clinics in the Park are at Ngoma and Chunga and there is a hospital at the Itezhi-Tezhi dam site. It is not advisable to drink unboiled water from the rivers and lagoons. Always keep your car windows closed when monkeys are around. Do your best to avoid being bitten by mosquitoes or tsetse flies. These flies can be a serious nuisance in some places where you are advised to keep your car windows closed.

All travellers should visit either their personal physician or a travel health clinic 4-8 weeks before departure for advice on health matters. Malaria prophylaxis with Lariam (mefloquine), Malarone (atovaquone/proguanil) or doxycycline is recommended for all areas, but expert medical

Hepatitis A	Recommended for all travellers
Typhoid	Recommended for all travellers
Polio	One-time booster recommended for any adult traveller who completed the childhood series but never had polio vaccine as an adult
Hepatitis B	Recommended for all travellers
Yellow fever	Recommended only for those who are travelling to the North West and Western Provinces and who are at risk for a large number of mosquito bites. South Africa is insisting that travellers that transit or live in South Africa and visit Zambia must have yellow fever vaccination, irrespective of how long they are in the country and where they go
Rabies	For travellers spending a lot of time outdoors, or at high risk for animal bites, or involved in any activities that might bring them into direct contact with bats
Measles, mumps, rubella (MMR)	Two doses recommended for all travellers born after 1956, if not previously given
Tetanus-diphtheria	Revaccination recommended every 10 years

advice should be taken before starting with any prophylactic. The vaccinations recommended in the box above are optional unless otherwise indicated. Visitors should see *www.mdtravelhealth.com/destinations/africa/zambia* for further information.

ZAWA Wildlife Police Officer.

Please remember that animals have right of way and although most will keep their distance or run away, there may be occasions when you meet potentially dangerous animals and you should not panic but exercise due caution. Be alert and be very careful when elephant, lion, leopard, buffalo, hippo and crocodile are around and of course beware of snakes that can appear at any time. Most animals will try to avoid you, but elephant and lion can be aggressive and it is best to give them a wide berth, especially when they are in a breeding group with young – let them pass if they are moving across your track, but back up if there is any sign that they are disturbed and want to come towards you. Under such circumstances move away slowly and keep a reasonable distance, always remaining in your car. If you are on a walking safari, pay careful attention to your guide and be sure to follow his instructions or signals.

You should book in and out of lodges and camps so that accidents, breakdowns or other mishaps can be sorted out with the minimum of delay. Radio communications still have many gaps. Lodges and ZAWA area managers only have bare essentials for breakdown assistance. Towing or vehicle recovery can sometimes be arranged, with the cost to be borne by the visitor. Mostly it is advisable to ensure that your bookings are made with lodges, giving them details of your planned routes and times of arrival so that they can monitor your trips and provide rescue assistance if necessary. Our advice is to be as self-contained as possible, making sure that you are well covered by your travel insurance for emergencies and rescue by special services. Good maps, a GPS and satellite phone will all help in maintaining your safety in an environment where radio communications are inadequate and there are big distances between hospitals and clinics. Communication systems are improving, as are sign posts and information, but we advise you to plan carefully and take common sense precautions along the lines we have suggested.

MAIN ITEMS TO REMEMBER

Hat
Jacket or thick pullover
Sunglasses
Binoculars
Camera
GPS
Maps
Cool box
Matches
Torch
Swiss Army Knife
First Aid kit
Sunscreen
Mosquito/insect repellent
Satellite phone
Insurance

FOOD AND EQUIPMENT

Much depends upon how long you are planning to be away from home and where you expect to stay. All the safari lodges, camps and bush camps are fully equipped, but the camping sites vary in the equipment and services they offer. Generally for campers conditions are basic although a few sites do have good facilities, but if not they can sometimes be improved by

Attendant at Total fuel station en route to Kafue National Park.

VITAL EQUIPMENT FOR SELF-DRIVE 4X4 JOURNEYS

All vehicle documents and handbook
Road tax, insurance, carbon tax
Driving licence
Maps showing waypoints
GPS
Satellite phone with charger system
Tent
Fridge
Two spare tyres
Two batteries
Full tool kit
Small compressor
Enough fuel
Water
High-lift jack (don't forget that your vehicle must have jacking points to fit)
Tow rope
Axe
Shovel

arrangement with the lodge if the campsite happens to be attached to one. There are few, if any, places after you leave the last town on your route where you can buy anything other than very limited items such as soap, candles, tea, salt, sugar, biscuits, cooking oil and a few vegetables and fruit etc. If you are intending to camp, then you should take everything that you will need. You will be told at the lodges whether the water is drinkable and if not then drinking water is always made available. It is better to play safe and ensure that you take some bottled water with you and if you are camping, then bring water purifying tablets or filtering equipment and in any case always boil your drinking water if possible. There is no fuel available in the Park. The last fuel on the M9 main road from Lusaka to Nalusanga gate is at the Total filling station in Mumbwa and when travelling from Livingstone to Dundumwezi the last fuel is at the Kobil station in Kalomo, just before the turning to the Park off the main T1 highway.

Although it is usually warm during the day, on some occasions there are strong cool breezes and nights can be very cold especially during June – September, so that it is wise to carry a light jacket, pullover and rug with you. Early morning and night drives in open safari cars can be very cold indeed and sitting by the campfire can often be a chilly experience for your back! Also, it is worth remembering that wearing a long-sleeved shirt will protect you from sunburn and insect bites, as well as keeping you warm in the evening.

For self-drivers, there are several car rental agencies that offer 4x4 vehicles for use in Zambia. If you choose this way to come to KNP, then it is essential that you are physically fit and really well equipped. The most important pieces of advice are to plan carefully, make sure you have appropriate travel insurance, bring along any personal items you think you will need on your trip and do not count on being able to find things that you have forgotten once you left the last town on your chosen route.

If you are interested in the night sky, Kafue is often clear and cloudless with a myriad of stars to gaze at; so bring along a "Planisphere" for the southern hemisphere that will help you identify the stars and constellations that traverse the entire heaven and will add so much fun to your trip. Planispheres are quite cheaply obtainable at many bookstores.

Fishing tackle is available at some of the lodges, but it is better to bring your own; light lures and lines, up to 5 kg breaking strain for bream and pike and heavier, 10 kg line or more for barbel. Fly fishing is always rewarding and flies with a white hackle that can be fished below the surface are recommended for bream, even in the late evenings. There are stockists in Lusaka and Livingstone. The most comprehensive variety of tackle is to be found at Tackle and Pet Haven, Shop No. 8 Manda Hill Centre, Lusaka. Phone: +260.211.251-088.

BANKING AND CURRENCY

The local currency is Kwacha (ZMW), with the notes in denominations of ZMW 100, 50, 20, 10, 5 and coins in denominations of ZMW 1, and 50n (ngwee), 10n and 5n. Exchange of foreign currency is carried out at authorised banks and bureaux de change. Most hotels, restaurants, travel agents and bigger shops accept credit cards. ATMs are available within Lusaka and some of the major towns. Standard Chartered and Barclays Bank have ATMs that accept Visa. Traveller's Cheques are widely accepted, but you may be required to show personal identification plus the original TC purchase bank's documentation.

Banking hours vary from bank to bank, but most are open Monday-Friday 08h15 to 14h30, with some opening from 08h15 to 10h30 on the first and last Saturday of the month.

At the time of going to press, the Zambian Kwacha, in line with other emerging market currencies, was suffering its biggest sell-off in a decade. These dramatic falls are driven mainly by investers' flight to safety to the US dollar in light of the euro crisis. Exchange rates have become particularly volatile, and

KNP main road signpost.

visitors are urged to check the latest information available from a reputable website currency converter, such as *www.oanda.com/currency/converter/.*

Although the law prohibits tipping as an informal rule it is, in fact, expected in most circumstances. In any case a 10% gratuity is usually added to the bill at many hotels and lodges in Zambia, which serves much the same purpose. If you are particularly satisfied by the service and attention that you receive from your driver or safari guide, then it is accepted practice that some extra expression of appreciation of friendliness and good work can be provided through a casual tip of around US$5-10 per person for a full day on safari - but this is entirely up to you.

BOOKINGS, ENQUIRIES AND USEFUL CONTACTS

All bookings and enquiries should be made through lodge or camp operators and the Kafue Park Operators' Association or the Zambia Wildlife Authority in Lusaka. Enquiries regarding Park administration or management and requests for entry permits for official visitors or research work should be directed to the Director General, ZAWA, Private Bag 1, Chilanga or the Regional Manager, ZAWA Western Region, Mumbwa. The Zambia Tourism Board is the national tourism body under the Ministry of Information, Broadcasting and Tourism that aims to promote Zambia as a tourist destination within and outside Zambia. It has offices that can provide much general information about travel in Zambia located in Lusaka (Head Office), Livingstone, Pretoria, Washington and London. Contact details:

Lusaka: 1st Floor Petroda House,
Great East Road, Lusaka, Zambia.
Phone: +260.211.229-087/90;
Fax: +260.211.225-174;
ztb@zambiatourism.org.zm;
www.zambiatourism.com

Livingstone: Zambia Tourist Centre, Box 603432, Livingstone, Zambia. Phone: +260.213.321-404/5; Fax: +260.213.321-487; *livingstone@zambiatourism.org.zm*

Pretoria: 570 Ziervogel St, (off Hamilton St), Arcadia, Box 12234, Hatfield 0083, Pretoria, South Africa. Phone: +27.12.326-1847 / 326-1854: Fax: +27.12. 326-2140 *zambiatourism@iburst.co.za* or *tourism@zambiapretoria.net*

London: Zambia High Commission, 2 Palace Gate, Kensington, London, W8 5NG, UK Phone: +44.207.589-6655; Fax: +44.207.581-1353; *ztb@aol.com*

Washington: 2419 Massuchetts Avenue, NW Washington, DC 2008, USA. *Phone: +1.202.265-9717; Fax: +1.202.332-0826; znt busa@aol.com*

Some other useful addresses

Department of Immigration Headquarters
Kent Building, Haile Selassie Road,
P.O. Box 50300, Lusaka.
Phone: +260.211.252-622/252-659
immighq@zamnet.zm/zambiavisa@zamnet.zm

Zambia Wildlife Authority (ZAWA) Headquarters
Director General, ZAWA, Kafue Road, Private Bag 1, Chilanga. *www.zawa.org.zm*
Phone: +260.211.278-080/129; *info@zawa.org.zm*

ZAWA Livingstone
Area Warden, Zambia Wildlife Authority, Mosi-o-Tunya Management Unit, Box 60086, Livingstone.
Phone: +260.213.322-213/321-396;
smalungo@zamnet.zm

ZAWA Mumbwa
Regional Manager, Western Region Office, Mumbwa. Phone: +260.211.800-056; mobile: +260.97.710-6559; *james_milanzi@yahoo.com*

Kafue Park Operators' Association – KPOA
The Chairman, Private Bag E523, Lusaka, Zambia.
Phone: +260.97.780-0651; *kafuenpoa@gmail.com*

The Kafue Trust
Fig Tree House, Warthog Road, Box 320181, Kabulonga, Lusaka, Zambia.
Phone: +260.211.262-773; mobile: +260.97.762-0323; *info@kafue.org*; *www.kafuetrust.org*

Open Africa
35 Wilderness Road, Box 44814, Claremont 7735, South Africa.
Phone: +27.21.683-9639; Fax: +27.21.683-8013; *admin@openafrica.org*

BirdWatch Zambia
Plot 13, Chindo Road, Box 33944, Woodlands, Lusaka, Zambia.
Phone: +260.211.260-709/255-981;
zos@zamnet.zm
www.wattledcrane.com

Car hire companies
Hemingways
P. O. Box 60810, Livingstone, Zambia.
Phone: +260.213.323-097; Mobile:+260 977.866-492/ +260.977.870-232;
info@hemingwayszambia.com
www.selfdrivezambia.com

Limo Hire Zambia
Lilayi Road, P. O. Box 65, Fringilla, Zambia.
Phone: +260.211278-628; mobile: +260.977.743-145
limohirezambia@gmail.com/
info@limohire-zambia.com
www.limo-hirezambia.com

Voyagers Travel and Tours, Lusaka.
Phone +260.211.253-064-5/082-4
lusaka@voyagerszambia.com
www.voyagerszambia.com

Voyagers Car Rental, Livingstone, Zambia.
Phone: +260.213.322-753;
carrental@voyagerszambia.com

ADDITIONAL READING

Benson, C.W., Brooke, R.K., Dowsett, R.J. & Irwin, M.P.S. 1971. *The Birds of Zambia*. Collins, London.

Blundell, M. 1987. *Collins Guide to the Wild Flowers of East Africa*. Collins, London.

Brammer, H. 1973. *Soils of Zambia 1971-1973*. Soil Survey Unit, Mount Makulu Research Station, Chilanga.

Broadley, D.G. 1971. The reptiles and amphibians of Zambia. *Puku* 6:1-143.

Coates Palgrave, K. 2006. *Trees of Southern Africa*. Struik, Cape Town.

d'Elbee, F. 2004. *Busanga*. Olpan, Paris.

Derricourt, R. 1985. *Man on the Kafue*. Ethnographica, London.

Dorst, J. & Dandelot, P. 1985. *A Field Guide to the Larger Mammals of Africa*. Collins, London.

Dowsett, R.J., Aspinwall, D.R. & Dowsett-Lemair, F. 2008. *The Birds of Zambia: An Atlas and Handbook*. Turaco Press.

Hockey, P.A.R., Dean, W.R.J. & Ryan, P.J. (eds). 2005. *Roberts – Birds of Southern Africa. VIIth edition*. The Trustees of the John Voelcker Bird Book Fund, Cape Town

Jackson, P.B.N. 1961. *The Fishes of Northern Rhodesia*. Government Printer, Lusaka.

Kingdon, J. 2004. *The Kingdon Pocket Guide to African Mammals*. D&N Publishing.

Leonard, P. 2005. *Important Bird Areas in Zambia*. The Zambian Ornithological Society, Lusaka.

Newman, K. 1983. *The Birds of Southern Africa*. Collins, London.

Pinhey, E.C.G. & Loe, I.D. 1973. *The Insects of Zambia*. Anglo American Corporation, Zambia.

Pinhey, E.C.G. & Loe, I.D. 1977. *The Butterflies of Zambia*. Anglo American Corporation, Zambia.

Sinclair, I. & Ryan, P. 2003. *Birds of Africa South of the Sahara*. Struik, Cape Town.

Skelton, P. (ed). 2001. *A Complete Guide to Freshwater Fishes of Southern Africa*. Struik, Cape Town.

Skinner, J.D. & Chimimba, C.T. 2005. The *Mammals of the Southern African Subregion*. Cambridge University Press, Cape Town.

CHECKLISTS OF WILDLIFE & COMMON TREES

The colloquial (common) and scientific names are included in all the checklists to help readers find the species they are looking for. Colloquial names differ from country to country and change with time. Every effort has been made to reflect modern usage and nomenclature. When there are accepted and well-used colloquial names, a second name is given in brackets. The lists are based upon the sources quoted at the end of Chapter 5. Any additions, comments or corrections should be sent to the Chairman of the Kafue Trust *(info@kafuetrust.org)*.

For the larger mammals and all of the birds, a "spotting checklist" has been included to the right of the names for your use for one day to a full week of "spotting", with a space to record the area of the KNP or the camp area where you made the sighting. For all the other lists, where sightings will in most cases be much more difficult, a single column has been inserted for your use.

Opposite: The fish-eagle in flight symbolises the freedom in Zambia and is its National Bird.

Below: Second in size only to the eland, the roan is found throughout the Park and the chances of encountering them are very good.

LARGER MAMMALS

Locality							
Days	1	2	3	4	5	6	7
Aardvark *Orycteropus afer*							
Aardwolf *Proteles cristata*							
Baboon, Chacma *Papio hamadryus*							
Baboon, Yellow *Papio cynocephalus*							
Buffalo, African *Syncerus caffer*							
Bushbaby, Thick-tailed (Greater Galago) *Otelmur crassicaudatus*							
Bushbuck *Tragelaphus scriptus*							
Bushpig *Potamochoerus larvatus*							
Caracal *Caracal caracal*							
Cat, African Wild *Felis silvestris*							
Cheetah *Acinonyx jubatus*							
Civet, African *Civettictis civetta*							
Dog, African Wild *Lycaon pictus*							
Duiker, Blue *Philantomba monticola*							
Duiker, Common *Sylvicapra grimmia*							
Duiker, Yellow-backed *Cephalophus silvicultor*							
Eland *Taurotragus oryx*							
Elephant, African *Loxodonta africana*							
Genet, Angolan *Genetta angolensis*							
Genet, Large-spotted *Genetta tigrina*							
Genet, Small-spotted *Genneta genetta*							
Grysbok, Sharpe's *Raphicerus sharpei*							

Hare, Scrub *Lepus saxatilis*							
Hartebeest, Lichtenstein's *Alcelaphus lichtensteinii*							
Hippopotamus *Hippopotamus amphibious*							
Honey badger (Ratel) *Mellivora capensis*							
Hyaena, Spotted *Crocuta crocuta*							
Hyrax (Dassie), Yellow-spotted (Rock) *Heterohyrax brucei*							
Hyrax (Dassie), Tree *Dendrohyrax arboreus*							
Impala *Aepyceros melampus*							
Jackal, Side-striped *Canis adustus*							
Klipspringer *Oreotragus oreotragus*							
Kudu *Tragelaphus strepsiceros*							
Lechwe, Red *Kobus leche*							
Leopard *Panthera pardus*							
Lion *Panthera leo*							
Mongoose, Banded *Mungos mungo*							
Mongoose, Dwarf *Helogale parvula*							
Mongoose, Large grey *Herpestes ichneumon*							
Mongoose, Marsh *Atilax paludinosis*							
Mongoose, Meller's *Rhynchogale melleri*							
Mongoose, Selous' *Paracynictus selousi*							
Mongoose, Slender *Galerella sanguinea*							
Mongoose, White-tailed *Ichneumia albicauda*							
Monkey, Vervet *Cercopithecus pygerythrus*							
Oribi *Ourebia ourebi*							
Otter, Clawless *Aonyx capensis*							
Otter, Spotted-necked *Lutra maculicollis*							
Pangolin, Ground *Manis temminckii*							
Polecat, Striped (Zorilla) *Ictonyx striatus*							
Porcupine, Cape *Hystrix africaeaustralis*							
Puku *Kobus vardoni*							
Reedbuck *Redunca arundinum*							
Roan Antelope *Hippotragus equinus*							
Sable Antelope *Hippotragus niger*							

Serval *Leptailurus serval*							
Sitatunga *Tregalaphus spekii*							
Springhare *Pedetes capensis*							
Steenbok (Steinbok) *Raphicerus campestris*							
Warthog *Phacochoerus africanus*							
Waterbuck, Common *Kobus ellipsiprymnus ellipsiprymnus*							
Waterbuck, Defassa *Kobus ellipsiprymnus defassa*							
Weasel, African striped *Poecilogale albinucha*							
Wildebeest, Blue *Connochaetes taurinus*							
Zebra, Plains *Equus quagga*							

The yellow-bellied house bat is one of 48 species of bats recorded from the KNP, and is widespread throughout the Park.

SMALLER MAMMALS	
Bat, African straw-coloured fruit *Eidolon helvum*	
Bat, Anchieta's pipistrelle *Hypsugo anchietai*	
Bat, Angolan free-tailed *Mops condylurus*	
Bat, Ansorge's free-tailed *Chaerephon ansorgei*	
Bat, Banana *Neoramicia nana*	
Bat, Blasius's horseshoe *Rhinolophus blasii*	
Bat, Botswana long-eared *Laephotis botswanae*	
Bat, Bushveld horseshoe *Rhinolophus simulator*	
Bat, Cape serotine *Neoromicia capensis*	
Bat, Damara woolly *Kerivoula argentata*	
Bat, Dark-winged lesser house *Scotoecus hindei/albigula*	
Bat, Darling's horseshoe *Rhinolophus darlingi*	
Bat, Dobson's epauletted fruit *Epomops dobsonii*	
Bat, Dusky pipistrelle *Pipistrellus hesperidus*	
Bat, Egyptian free-tailed *Tadarida aegyptiaca*	
Bat, Egyptian rousette *Rousettus aegyptiacus*	
Bat, Egyptian slit-faced *Nycteris thebasica*	
Bat, Giant leaf-nosed *Hipposideros gigas*	
Bat, Green house *Scotophilus viridis*	
Bat, Hairy slit-faced *Nycteris hispida*	
Bat, Hilderbrandt's horseshoe *Rhinolophus hilderbrandtii*	
Bat, Lander's horseshoe *Rhinolophus landeri*	
Bat, Large-eared slit-faced *Nycteris macrotis*	
Bat, Lesser woolly *Kerivoula lanosa*	
Bat, Little free-tailed *Chaerephon pumilus*	
Bat, Long-tailed serotine *Eptesicus hottentotus*	
Bat, Mauritian tomb *Taphozous mauritianus*	
Bat, Midas free-tailed *Mops midas*	
Bat, Natal long-fingered *Miniopterus natalensis*	
Bat, Nigerian free-tailed *Chaerephon nigeriae*	
Bat, Noack's leaf-nosed *Hipposideros ruber*	

Bat, Percival's short-eared trident *Cloetis percivali*		
Bat, Peter's epauletted fruit *Epomorphorus crypturus*		
Bat, Rendall's seratine *Neoromicia rendalli*		
Bat, Ruppell's pipistrelle *Pipistrellus ruppelli*		
Bat, Ruppell's horseshoe *Rhinolophus fumigatus*		
Bat, Rusty pipistrelle *Pipistrellus rusticus*		
Bat, Schlieffen's twilight *Nycticeinops schlieffeni*		
Bat, Striped leaf-nosed *Hipposideros vittatus*		
Bat, Sundevall's leaf-nosed *Hipposideros caffer*		
Bat, Swinny's horseshoe *Rhinolophus swinnyi*		
Bat, Thomas's flat-headed *Mimetillus thomasi*		
Bat, Variegated butterfly *Glauconycteris variegata*		
Bat, Wahlberg's epauletted fruit *Epomophorus wahlbergi*		
Bat, White-bellied free-tailed *Mops niveiventer*		
Bat, White-bellied house *Scotophilus leucogaster*		
Bat, Yellow-bellied house *Scotophilus dinganii*		
Bat, Zulu serotine *Neoromicia zuluensis*		
Canerat, Greater *Thryonomys swinderianus*		
Canerat, Lesser *Thryonomys gregorianus*		
Dormouse, Johnston's African *Graphiurus johnstoni*		
Dormouse, Rock *Graphiurus platyops*		
Dormouse, Woodland *Graphiurus murinus*		
Elephant-Shrew, Four-toed *Petrodromus tetradactylus*		
Elephant-Shrew, Short-snouted *Elephantulus brachyrhynchus*		
Gerbil, Boehm's *Tatera boehmi*		
Gerbil, Bushveld *Tatera leucogaster*		
Gerbil, Savanna *Tatera valida*		
Hedgehog, African *Atelerix albiventris*		
Mole-Rat, African *Cryptomys hottentotus*		
Mole-Rat, Giant *Cryptomys mechowi*		
Mouse, Angolan wood *Otomys angolensis*		
Mouse, Brandt's climbing *Dendromus mesomelas*		
Mouse, Chestnut climbing *Dendromus mystacalis*		

Mouse, Fat *Steatomys minutus & pratensis*	
Mouse, Grey-bellied pygmy *Mus triton*	
Mouse, Grey climbing *Dendromus melanotis*	
Mouse, Griselda's striped grass *Lemniscomys griselda*	
Mouse, Hildergarde's broad-headed *Zelotomys hildegardeae*	
Mouse, Kreb's fat *Steatomys krebsi*	
Mouse, Natal multimammate *Mastomys natalensis*	
Mouse, Nyika climbing *Dendromus nyikae*	
Mouse, Pouched *Saccostomus campestris*	
Mouse, Pygmy *Mus minutoides*	
Mouse, Spiny *Acomys spinosissimus*	
Mouse, Thomas's pygmy *Mus sorella*	
Mouse, Woodland *Thamnomys dolichurus*	
Night Ape (Lesser Galago) *Galago moholi*	
Rat, Acacia *Thallomys paedulcus*	
Rat, African grass *Arvicanthis niloticus*	
Rat, Creek grooved-tooth *Pelomys fallax*	
Rat, Giant-pouched (Gambian) *Cricetomys gambianus*	
Rat, Kaiser's rock *Aethomys kaiseri*	
Rat, Nyika rock *Aethomys nyikae*	
Rat, Red veld *Aethomys chrysophilus*	
Shrew, Greater dwarf *Suncus lixus*	
Shrew, Giant musk *Crocidura olivieri*	
Shrew, Lesser red musk *Crocidura hirta*	
Shrew, Peter's musk *Crocidura pitmani*	
Shrew, Reddish-grey musk *Crocidura parvipes*	
Shrew, Swamp musk *Crocidura mariquensis*	
Shrew, Tiny musk *Crocidura fuscomurina*	
Shrew, Tumultuous *Crocidura turba*	
Squirrel, Flying *Anomalurus derbianus*	
Squirrel, Sun *Heliosciurus gambianus*	
Squirrel, Tree *Paraxerus cepapi*	

BIRDS

Checklist includes both the Kafue National Park and adjacent Game Management Areas.

Locality							
Days	1	2	3	4	5	6	7
Akalat, Bocage's *Sheppardia bocagei*							
Apalis, Brown-headed *Apalis alticola*							
Apalis, Yellow-breasted *Apalis flavida*							
Avocet, Pied *Recurvirostra avosetta*							
Babbler, Arrow-marked *Turdoides jardineii*							
Babbler, Hartlaub's *Turdoides hartlaubsii*							
Barbet, Anchieta's *Stactolaema anchietae*							
Barbet, Black-backed *Lybius minor*							
Barbet, Black-collared *Lybius torquatus*							
Barbet, Chaplin's (Zambian) *Lybius chaplini*							
Barbet, Crested *Trachyphonus vaillantii*							
Barbet, Miombo pied *Tricholaema frontata*							
Bateleur *Terathopius ecaudatus*							
Batis, Chinspot *Batis molitor*							
Batis, Margaret's *Batis margaritae*							
Bee-eater, Blue-breasted *Merops variegatus*							
Bee-eater, Blue-cheeked *Merops persicus*							
Bee-eater, Böhm's *Merops boehmi*							
Bee-eater, European *Merops apiaster*							
Bee-eater, Little *Merops pusillus*							
Bee-eater, Southern carmine *Merops nubicoides*							
Bee-eater, Swallow-tailed *Merops hirundineus*							

Bee-eater, White-fronted *Merops bullockoides*							
Bishop, Black-winged (Fire-crowned) *Euplectes hordeaceus*							
Bishop, Southern red *Euplectes orix*							
Bishop, Yellow *Euplectes capensis*							
Bishop, Yellow-crowned (Golden) *Euplectes afer*							
Bittern, Dwarf *Ixobrychus sturmii*							
Bittern, Little *Ixobrychus minutus*							
Boubou, Tropical *Laniarius major*							
Broadbill, African *Smithornis capensis*							
Brownbul, Terrestrial *Phyllastrephus terrestris*							
Brubru *Nilaus afer*							
Buffalo-Weaver, Red-billed *Bubalornis niger*							
Bulbul, Dark-capped (Black-eyed) *Pyconotus tricolor*							
Bunting, Cabanis's *Embariza cabanisi*							
Bunting, Cinnamon-breasted (Rock) *Emberiza tahapisi*							
Bunting, Golden-breasted *Embariza flaviventris*							
Bush-Shrike, Black-fronted *Chlorophoneus multicolour*							
Bush-Shrike, Grey-headed *Malaconotus blanchoti*							
Bush-Shrike, Orange-breasted *Chlorophpneus sulfureopectus*							
Bustard, Black-bellied *Lisotis melanogaster*							
Bustard, Denham's (Stanley's) *Neotis denhami*							
Bustard, (Northern) White-bellied *Eupodotis senegalensis*							
Buttonquail, Black-rumped *Turnix nanus*							
Buttonquail, Kurrichane (Small) *Turnix sylvaticus*							
Buzzard, Common (Steppe) *Buteo buteo*							
Buzzard, European honey *Pernis apivorus*							
Buzzard, Lizard *Kaupifalco monogrammicus*							
Camaroptera, Grey-backed *Camaroptera brevicaudata*							
Canary, Black-thoated *Crithagra atrogularis*							
Canary, Brimstone (Bully) *Crithagra sulphurata*							
Canary, Yellow-fronted *Crithagra mozambica*							
Chat, Arnott's (White-headed black) *Pentholaea arnoti*							
Chat, Familiar *Oenanthe familiaris*							

Chat, Sooty *Myrmecocichla nigra*							
Cisticola, Chirping *Cisticola pipiens*							
Cisticola, Croaking *Cisticola natalensis*							
Cisticola, Desert *Cisticola aridulus*							
Cisticola, Levaillant's (Tinkling) *Cisticola tinniens*							
Cisticola, Luapula *Cisticola luapula*							
Cisticola, Pale-crowned *Cisticola cinnamomeus*							
Cisticola, Rattling *Cisticola chiniana*							
Cisticola, Red-faced *Cisticola erythrops*							
Cisticola, Rufous-winged *Cisticola galactotes*							
Cisticola, Short-winged (Siffling) *Cisticola brachypterus*							
Cisticola, Tinkling (Grey) *Cisticola rufilatus*							
Cisticola, Trilling *Cisticola woosnami*							
Cisticola, Zitting (Fan-tailed) *Cisticola juncidis*							
Cliff-Chat, Mocking *Thamnolaea cinnamomeiventris*							
Coot, Red-knobbed (Crested) *Fulica cristata*							
Cormorant, Reed (Long-tailed) *Microcarbo africanus*							
Cormorant, White-breasted *Phalacrocorax lucidus*							
Corncrake *Crex crex*							
Coucal, Black *Centropus grillii*							
Coucal, Burchell's *Centropus burchelli*							
Coucal, Coppery-tailed *Centropus cupreicaudus*							
Coucal, Senegal *Centropus senegalensis*							
Courser, Bronze-winged (Violet-tipped) *Rhinoptilus chalcopterus*							
Courser, Temminck's *Cursorius temminckii*							
Courser, Three-banded (Heuglin's) *Rhinoptilus cinctus*							
Crake, African *Crecopsis egregia*							
Crake, Black *Amaurornis flavirostra*							
Crake, Spotted *Porzana porzana*							
Crake, Striped *Aenigmatolimnas marginalis*							
Crane, Grey crowned *Balearica regulorum*							
Crane, Wattled *Bageranus carunculata*							
Creeper, Spotted *Salpornis spilonatus*							

Crombec, Long-billed *Sylvietta rufescens*							
Crombec, Red-capped *Sylvietta ruficapilla*							
Crow, Pied *Corvus albus*							
Cuckoo, African *Cuculus gularis*							
Cuckoo, African emerald *Cercococcyx cupreus*							
Cuckoo, Black *Cuculus clamosus*							
Cuckoo, Common (Eurasian) *Cuculus canorus*							
Cuckoo, Diderick *Chrysococcyx caprius*							
Cuckoo, Great spotted *Clamator glandarius*							
Cuckoo, Jacobin *Clamator jacobinus*							
Cuckoo, Klaas's *Chrysococcyx klaas*							
Cuckoo, Levaillant's (African striped) *Clamator levaillantii*							
Cuckoo, Red-chested *Cuculus solitarius*							
Cuckoo, Thick-billed *Pachycoccyx audeberti*							
Cuckooshrike, Black *Campephaga flava*							
Cuckooshrike, Purple-throated *Campephaga quiscalina*							
Cuckooshrike,White-breasted *Coracina pectoralis*							
Curlew, Eurasian *Numenius arquata*							
Darter, African *Anhinga rufa*							
Dove, African mourning *Streptopelia decipiens*							
Dove, Laughing (Palm) *Spilopelia senegalensis*							
Dove, Namaqua *Oena capensis*							
Dove, Red-eyed *Streptopelia semitorquata*							
Drongo, Fork-tailed *Dicrurus adsimilis*							
Drongo, Square-tailed *Dicrurus ludwigii*							
Duck, African Black *Anas sparsa*							
Duck, Comb (Knob-billed) *Sarkidiornis melanotos*							
Duck, Fulvous *Dendrocygna bicolor*							
Duck, White-backed *Thalassornis leuconotus*							
Duck, White-faced *Dendrocygna viduata*							
Duck, Yellow-billed *Anas undulata*							
Eagle, African crowned (Crowned hawk-) *Stephanoaetus coronatus*							
Eagle, Booted *Hieraatus pennatus*							

Eagle, Lesser spotted *Aquila pomarina*							
Eagle, Long-crested *Lophaetus occipitalis*							
Eagle, Martial *Polemaetus bellicosus*							
Eagle, Steepe *Aquila nipalensis*							
Eagle, Tawny *Aquila rapax*							
Eagle, Wahlberg's *Hieraaetus wahlbergi*							
Eagle-Owl, Spotted *Bubo africanus*							
Eagle-Owl, Verreaux's (Giant) *Bubo lacteus*							
Egret, Cattle *Bubulcus ibis*							
Egret, Great white *Ardea alba*							
Egret, Little *Egretta garzetta*							
Egret, Slaty *Egretta vinaceigula*							
Egret, Yellow-billed (Intermediate) *Egretta intermedia*							
Eremomela, Black-necked *Eremomela atricollis*							
Eremomela, Burnt-necked *Eremomela usticollis*							
Eremomela, Green-capped *Eremomela scotops*							
Eremomela, Yellow-bellied *Eremomela icteropygialis*							
Falcon, Amur (Eastern red-footed) *Falco amurensis*							
Falcon, Lanner *Falco biarmicus*							
Falcon, Peregrine *Falco peregrinus*							
Falcon, (Western) Red-footed *Falco vespertinus*							
Falcon, Red-necked *Falco chicquera*							
Finch, Cuckoo *Anamalospiza imberbis*							
Finch, Cut-throat *Amadina fasciata*							
Finfoot, African *Podica senegalensis*							
Firefinch, African (Blue-billed) *Lagonosticta rubricata*							
Firefinch, Brown *Lagonosticta nitidula*							
Firefinch, Jameson's *Lagonosticta rhodopareia*							
Firefinch, Red-billed *Lagonosticta senegala*							
Fish-eagle, African *Haliaeetus vocifer*							
Fishing-Owl, Pel's *Scotopelia peli*							
Flamingo, Lesser *Pheoniconaias minor*							
Flufftail, Buff-spotted *Sarothrura elegans*							

Flufftail, Red-chested *Sarothrura rufa*							
Flufftail, Streaky-breasted *Sarothrura boehmi*							
Flycatcher, African dusky *Muscicapa adusta*							
Flycatcher, Ashy (Blue-grey) *Muscicapa caerulescens*							
Flycatcher, Blue-mantled crested *Trochocercus cyanomelas*							
Flycatcher, Böhm's *Muscicapa boehmi*							
Flycatcher, Collared *Ficedula albicollis*							
Flycatcher, Pale (Mouse-coloured) *Bradornis pallidus*							
Flycatcher, Southern black *Melaenornis pammelaina*							
Flycatcher, Spotted *Muscicapa striata*							
Flycatcher, White-tailed blue *Elminia albicauda*							
Francolin, Coqui *Peliperdix coqui*							
Francolin, Crested *Dendroperdix sephaena*							
Francolin, Shelley's *Scleroptila shelleyi*							
Gallinule, Purple (African purple swamphen) *Porphyrio madagascariensis*							
Gallinule, Allen's (Lesser) *Porphyrio alleni*							
Go-away-bird (Lourie), Grey *Corythaixoides concolor*							
Goose, African pygmy *Nettapus auritus*							
Goose, Egyptian *Alopochen aegyptiaca*							
Goose, Spur-winged *Plectropterus gambensis*							
Goshawk, African *Accipiter tachiro*							
Goshawk, Dark chanting *Melierax metabates*							
Goshawk, Gabar *Micronisus gabar*							
Grassbird, Fan-tailed (Broad-tailed Warbler) *Schoenicola brevirostris*							
Grass-Owl, African *Tyto capensis*							
Grebe, Little (Dabchick) *Tachybaptus ruficollis*							
Greenbul, Cabanis's *Phyllastrephus cabanisi*							
Greenbul, Grey-olive *Phyllastrephus cerviniventris*							
Greenbul, Yellow-bellied *Chlorocichla flaviventris*							
Greenshank, Common *Tringa nebularia*							
Ground-Hornbill, Southern *Bucorvus leadbeateri*							
Guineafowl, Crested *Guttera pucherani*							
Guineafowl, Helmeted *Numida meleagris*							

Gull, Grey-headed *Chroicocephalus cirrocephalus*							
Gull, Lesser black-backed *Larus fuscus*							
Hammerkop *Scopus umbretta*							
Harrier, Montagu's *Circus pygargus*							
Harrier, Pallid *Circus macrourus*							
Harrier-Hawk, African (Gymnogene) *Polyboroides typus*							
Hawk, African cuckoo *Aviceda cuculoides*							
Hawk, Bat *Macheiramphus alcinus*							
Hawk-Eagle, African *Aquila spilogaster*							
Hawk-Eagle, Ayres's *Hieraaetus ayresii*							
Helmet-Shrike, Retz's (Red-billed) *Prionops retzii*							
Helmet-Shrike, White-crested *Prionops plumatus*							
Heron (Egret), Black *Egretta ardesiaca*							
Heron, Black-headed *Ardea melanocephala*							
Heron, Goliath *Ardea goliath*							
Heron, Green-backed *Butorides striata*							
Heron, Grey *Ardea cinerea*							
Heron, Purple *Ardea purpurea*							
Heron, Rufous-bellied *Ardeola rufiventris*							
Heron, Squacco *Ardeola ralloides*							
Hobby, African *Falco cuvierii*							
Hobby, Eurasian *Falco subbuteo*							
Honeybird, Brown-backed (Sharp-billed Honeyguide) *Prodotiscus regulus*							
Honeybird, Green-backed (Slender-billed Honeyguide) *Prodotiscus zambesiae*							
Honeyguide, Greater *Indicator indicator*							
Honeyguide, Lesser *Indicator minor*							
Honeyguide, Scaly-throated *Indicator variegatus*							
Hoopoe, African *Upupa Africana*							
Hornbill, African grey *Tockus nasutus*							
Hornbill, Crowned *Tockus alboterminatus*							
Hornbill, Pale-billed *Tockus pallidirostris*							
Hornbill, Southern red-billed *Tockus rufirostris*							
Hornbill, Southern yellow-billed *Tockus leucomelas*							

Hornbill, Trumpeter *Bycanistes bucinator*							
Hyliota, Southern (Mashona) *Hyliota australis*							
Hyliota, Yellow-bellied *Hyliota flavigaster*							
Ibis, African sacred *Threskiornis aethiopicus*							
Ibis, Glossy *Plegadis falcinellus*							
Ibis, Hadada *Bostrychia hagedash*							
Indigobird, Dusky (Variable) (Black Widowfinch) *Vidua funerea*							
Indigobird, Purple (Purple Widowfinch) *Vidua purpurascens*							
Indigobird, Village (Steel-blue Widowfinch) *Vidua chalybeata*							
Jacana, African *Actophilornis africanus*							
Jacana, Lesser *Microparra capensis*							
Kestrel, Common *Falco tinnunculus*							
Kestrel, Dickinson's *Falco dickinsoni*							
Kestrel, Greater *Falco rupicoloides*							
Kestrel, Lesser *Falco naumanni*							
Kingfisher, Brown-hooded *Halcyon albiventris*							
Kingfisher, Giant *Megaceryle maxima*							
Kingfisher, Grey-headed *Halycon leucocephala*							
Kingfisher, Half-collared *Alcedo semitorquata*							
Kingfisher, Malachite *Corythornis cristatus*							
Kingfisher, Pied *Ceryle rudis*							
Kingfisher, Striped *Halycon chelicuti*							
Kingfisher, Woodland *Halycon senegalensis*							
Kite, Black *Milvus migrans*							
Kite, Black-shouldered *Elanus caeruleus*							
Kite, Yellow-billed *Milvus aegyptius*							
Kooran, Red-chested *Lophotis ruficrista*							
Lapwing (Plover), African wattled *Vanellus senegallus*							
Lapwing (Plover), Blacksmith *Vanellus armatus*							
Lapwing (Plover), Crowned *Vanellus coronatus*							
Lapwing (Plover), Long-toed *Vanellus crassirostris*							
Lapwing (Plover), Senegal (Lesser black-winged) *Vanellus lugubris*							
Lapwing (Plover), White-headed (White-crowned) *Vanellus albiceps*							

Lark, Dusky *Pinarocorys nigricans*							
Lark, Flappet *Mirafra rufocinnamomea*							
Lark, Red-capped *Calandrella cinerea*							
Lark, Rufous-naped *Mirafra africana*							
Locustfinch *Paludipasser locustella*							
Longclaw, Fulleborn's *Macronyx fuelleborni*							
Longclaw, Rosy-breasted (Pink-throated) *Macronyx ameliae*							
Lovebird, Black-cheeked *Agapornis nigrigenis*							
Mannikin, Black-and-white *Lonchura bicolor*							
Mannikin, Bronze *Lonchura cucullata*							
Mannikin, Magpie (Pied) *Lonchura fringilloides*							
Marsh-Harrier, African *Circus ranivorus*							
Marsh-Harrier, Western (Eurasian) *Circus aeruginosus*							
Martin, Banded *Riparia cincta*							
Martin, Brown-throated (Plain) *Riparia paludicola*							
Martin, Common house *Delichon urbicum*							
Martin, Rock *Ptonoprogne fuligula*							
Martin, Sand *Riparia riparia*							
Moorhen, Common *Gallinula chloropus*							
Moorhen, Lesser *Gallinula angulate*							
Mousebird, Red-faced *Urocolius indicus*							
Neddicky (Piping Cisticola) *Cisticola fulvicapilla*							
Night-Heron, White-backed *Gorsachius leuconotus*							
Night-Heron, Black-crowned *Nycticorax nycticorax*							
Nightingale, Thrush *Luscinia luscinia*							
Nightjar, Eurasian *Caprimulgus europaeus*							
Nightjar, Fiery-necked *Caprimulgus pectoralis*							
Nightjar, Freckled *Caprimulgus tristigma*							
Nightjar, Pennant-winged *Macrodipteryx vexillarius*							
Nightjar, Rufous-cheeked *Caprimulgus rufigena*							
Nightjar, Square-tailed (Mozambique) *Caprimulgus fossii*							
Nightjar, Swamp (Natal) *Caprimulgus natalensis*							
Openbill, African *Anastomus lamelligerus*							

Oriole, African golden *Oriolus auratus*							
Oriole, (Eastern) Black-headed *Oriolus larvatus*							
Oriole, Eurasian golden *Oriolus oriolus*							
Osprey, Western *Pandion haliaetus*							
Owl, Barn *Tyto alba*							
Owl, Marsh *Asio capensis*							
Owlet, African barred *Glaucidium capensis*							
Owlet, Pearl-spotted *Glaucidium perlatum*							
Oxpecker, Red-billed *Buphagus erythrorhynchus*							
Oxpecker, Yellow-billed *Buphagus africanus*							
Palm-Thrush, Collared *Cichladusa arquata*							
Paradise-Flycatcher, African *Terpsiphone viridis*							
Paradise-Whydah, Broad-tailed *Vidua obtusa*							
Paradise-Whydah, Long-tailed *Vidua paradisaea*							
Parrot, Grey-headed *Poicephalus suahelicus*							
Parrot, Meyer's (Brown) *Poicephalus meyeri*							
Pelican, Great white *Pelecanus onocrotalus*							
Pelican, Pink-backed *Pelecanus rufescens*							
Penduline-Tit, Grey (African) *Anthoscopus caroli*							
Petronia, Yellow-throated *Gymnoris superciliaris*							
Pigeon, African green *Treron calvus*							
Pipit, African (Grassveld) *Anthus cinnamomeus*							
Pipit, Buffy *Anthus vaalensis*							
Pipit, Bushveld *Anthus caffer*							
Pipit, Long-billed *Anthus similis*							
Pipit, Plain-backed *Anthus leucophrys*							
Pipit, Striped *Anthus lineiventris*							
Pipit, Tree *Anthus trivialis*							
Plover, Caspian *Charadrius asiaticus*							
Plover, Common ringed *Charadrius hiaticula*							
Plover, Grey (Black-bellied) *Pulvialis squatarola*							
Plover, Kittlitz's *Charadrius pecuarius*							
Plover, Three-banded *Charadrius tricollaris*							

Pochard, Southern *Netta erythrophthalma*							
Pratincole, Black-winged *Glareola nordmanni*							
Pratincole, Collared (Red-winged) *Glareola pratincola*							
Pratincole, Rock *Glareola nuchalis*							
Prinia, Tawny-flanked *Prinia subflava*							
Puffback, Black-backed *Dryoscopus cubla*							
Pygmy-Kingfisher, African *Ispidina picta*							
Pytilia, Green-winged (Melba Finch) *Pytilia melba*							
Pytilia, Orange-winged (Golden-backed) *Pytilia afra*							
Quail, Blue *Excalfactoria adansonii*							
Quail, Harlequin *Coturnix delegorguei*							
Quailfinch, African *Ortygospiza fuscocrissa*							
Quailfinch, Black-chinned *Ortygospiza gabonensis*							
Quelea, Red-billed *Quelea quelea*							
Quelea, Red-headed *Quelea erythrops*							
Rail, African *Rallus caerulescens*							
Redshank, Common *Tringa totanus*							
Redshank, Spotted *Tringa erythropus*							
Robin-chat, Red-capped (Natal) *Cossypha natalensis*							
Robin-chat, White-browed (Heuglin's) *Cossypha heuglini*							
Rock-Thrush, Miombo *Monticola angolensis*							
Roller, Broad-billed *Eurystomus glaucurus*							
Roller, European *Coracias garrulus*							
Roller, Lilac-breasted *Coracias caudatus*							
Roller, Purple (Rufous-crowned) *Coracias naevius*							
Roller, Racquet-tailed *Coracias spatulatus*							
Ruff *Philomachus pugnax*							
Sanderling *Calidris alba*							
Sandgrouse, Double-banded *Pterocles bicinctus*							
Sandgrouse, Yellow-throated *Pterocles gutturalis*							
Sandpiper, Common *Actitis hypoleucos*							
Sandpiper, Curlew *Calidris ferruginea*							
Sandpiper, Green *Tringa ochropus*							

Sandpiper, Marsh *Tringa stagnatilis*							
Sandpiper, Wood *Tringa glareola*							
Saw-wing, Black *Psalidoprocne pristoptera*							
Scimitarbill, Common *Rhinopomastus cyanomelas*							
Scops-Owl, African *Otus senegalensis*							
Scops-Owl, Southern white-faced *Ptilopsis granti*							
Scrub-Robin, Bearded *Erythropygia quadrivirgata*							
Scrub-Robin, Miombo (Central Bearded) *Erythropygia barbata*							
Scrub-Robin, White-browed *Erythropygia leucophrys*							
Secretary Bird *Sagittarius serpentarius*							
Seedeater, Black-eared *Crithagra mennelli*							
Seedeater, Reichard's (Stripe-breasted) *Crithagra reichardi*							
Shikra (Little-banded Goshawk) *Accipiter badius*							
Shoebill *Balaeniceps rex*							
Shrike, Common fiscal *Lanius collaris*							
Shrike, Lesser grey *Lanius minor*							
Shrike, Magpie (Long-tailed) *Urolestes melanoleucus*							
Shrike, Red-backed *Lanius collurio*							
Shrike, Sousa's *Lanius souzae*							
Skimmer, African *Rynchops flavirostris*							
Snake-Eagle, Black-chested *Circaetus pectoralis*							
Snake-Eagle, Brown *Circaetus cinereus*							
Snake-Eagle, Western banded *Circaetus cinerascens*							
Snipe, African (Ethiopian) *Gallinago nigripennis*							
Snipe, Great *Gallinago media*							
Snipe, Greater painted *Rostratula benghalensis*							
Sparrow, House *Passer domesticus*							
Sparrow, Northern grey-headed *Passer griseus*							
Sparrow, Southern grey-headed *Passer diffusus*							
Sparrowhawk, Black (Great) *Accipiter melanoleucus*							
Sparrowhawk, Little *Accipiter minullus*							
Sparrowhawk, Ovambo *Accipiter ovampensis*							
Sparrowlark, Chestnut-backed *Eremopterix leucotis*							

Sparrowlark, Grey-backed *Eremopterix verticalis*							
Sparrow-Weaver, Chestnut-backed *Plocepasser rufoscapulatus*							
Sparrow-Weaver, White-browed *Plocepasser mahali*							
Spinetail, Böhm's (Bat-like) *Neafrapus boehmi*							
Spoonbill, African *Platalea alba*							
Spurfowl (Francolin), Natal *Pternistis natalensis*							
Spurfowl (Francolin), Red-necked *Pternistis afer*							
Spurfowl (Francolin), Swainson's *Pternistis swainsonii*							
Starling, Greater blue-eared *Lamprotornis chalybaeus*							
Starling, Meve's *Lamprotornis mevesii*							
Starling, Miombo blue-eared *Lamprotornis elizabeth*							
Starling, Sharp-tailed *Lamprotornis acuticaudus*							
Starling, Splendid glossy *Lamprotornis splendidus*							
Starling, Violet-backed (Plum-coloured, Amethyst) *Cinnyricinclus leucogaster*							
Starling, Wattled *Creatophora cinerea*							
Stilt, Black-winged *Himantopus himantopus*							
Stint, Little *Calidris minuta*							
Stonechat, Common *Saxicola torquatus*							
Stork, Abdim's (White-bellied) *Ciconia abdimii*							
Stork, Marabou *Leptoptilos crumenifer*							
Stork, Saddle-billed *Ephippiorhynchus senegalensis*							
Stork, White *Ciconia ciconia*							
Stork, Wooly-necked *Ciconia episcopus*							
Stork, Yellow-billed *Mycteria ibis*							
Sunbird, Amethyst (Black) *Chalcomitra amethystina*							
Sunbird, Anchieta's (Red-and-blue) *Anthreptes anchietae*							
Sunbird, Collared *Hedydipna collaris*							
Sunbird, Copper (Coppery) *Cinnyris cupreus*							
Sunbird, Miombo double-collared *Cinnyris manoensis*							
Sunbird, Olive *Cyanomitra olivacea*							
Sunbird, Purple-banded *Cinnyris bifasciatus*							
Sunbird, Scarlet-chested *Chalcomitra senegalensis*							
Sunbird, Shelley's *Cinnyris shelleyi*							

Sunbird, Variable (Yellow-bellied) *Cinnyris venustus*							
Sunbird, Western violet-backed *Anthreptes longuemarei*							
Sunbird, White-bellied *Cinnyris talatala*							
Swallow, Barn (European) *Hirundo rustica*							
Swallow, Greater striped *Cecropis cucullata*							
Swallow, Grey-rumped *Pseudhirundo griseopyga*							
Swallow, Lesser striped *Cecropis abyssinica*							
Swallow, Mosque *Cecropis senegalensis*							
Swallow, Pearl-breasted *Hirundo dimidiate*							
Swallow, Red-breasted *Cecropis semirufa*							
Swallow, White-thoated *Hirundo albigularis*							
Swallow, Wire-tailed *Hirundo smithii*							
Swift, African Palm *Cypsiurus parvus*							
Swift, Common *Apus apus*							
Swift, Little *Apus affinis*							
Swift, White-rumped *Apus caffer*							
Teal, Hottentot *Anas hottentota*							
Teal, Red-billed *Anas erythrorhyncha*							
Tchagra, Black-crowned *Tchagra senegalus*							
Tchagra, Brown-crowned (Three-streaked) *Tchagra australis*							
Tchagra, Anchieta's *Bocagia anchietae*							
Tern, Gull-billed *Gelochelidon nilotica*							
Tern, Whiskered *Chlidonias hybrid*							
Tern, White-winged *Chlidonias leucopterus*							
Thick-knee (Dikkop), Spotted *Burhinus capensis*							
Thick-knee (Dikkop), Water *Burhinus vermiculatus*							
Thrush, African *Turdus pelios*							
Thrush, Groundscraper *Psophocichla litsitsirupa*							
Thrush, Kurrichane *Turdus libonyana*							
Tinkerbird, Yellow-rumped *Pogoniulus bilineatus*							
Tinkerbird, Yellow-fronted *Pogoniulus chrysoconus*							
Tit, Miombo *Parus griseiventris*							
Tit, Rufous-bellied *Parus rufiventris*							

Tit, Southern Black *Parus niger*							
Tit, White-winged Black *Parus leucomelas*							
Tit-babbler, Chestnut-vented *Sylvia subcaerulea*							
Tit-Flycatcher, Grey (Lead-coloured) *Myioparus plumbeus*							
Trogan, Narina *Apaloderma narina*							
Turaco, Ross's *Musophaga rossae*							
Turaco, Schalow's *Tauraco schalowi*							
Turtle-Dove, Cape (Ring-necked) *Streptopelia capicola*							
Twinspot, Red-throated (Peters's) *Hypargos niveoguttatus*							
Vulture, Cape *Gyps coprotheres*							
Vulture, Hooded *Necrosyrtes monachus*							
Vulture, Lappet-faced *Torgos tracheliotus*							
Vulture, White-backed *Gyps africanus*							
Vulture, White-headed *Trigonoceps occipitalis*							
Wagtail, African pied *Motacilla aguimp*							
Wagtail, Cape *Motacilla capensis*							
Wagtail, Yellow *Motacilla flava*							
Warbler, African reed (African marsh) *Acrocephalus baeticatus*							
Warbler, Dark-capped yellow *Iduna natalensis*							
Warbler, Eurasian reed *Acrocephalus scirpaceus*							
Warbler, Evergreen forest *Bradypterus lopezi*							
Warbler, Garden *Sylvia borin*							
Warbler, Great reed *Acrocephalus arundinaceus*							
Warbler, Greater swamp *Acrocephalus rufescens*							
Warbler, Icterine *Hippolais icterina*							
Warbler, Laura's woodland *Phylloscopus laurae*							
Warbler, Lesser swamp (Cape reed) *Acrocephalus gracilirostris*							
Warbler, Little rush (African sedge) *Bradypterus baboecala*							
Warbler, Marsh *Acrocephalus palustris*							
Warbler, Moustached Grass *Melocichla mentalis*							
Warbler, Sedge *Acrocephalus schoenobaenus*							
Warbler, Willow *Phylloscopus trochilus*							
Wattle-eye, Black-throated *Pltaysteira peltata*							

Waxbill, Blue (Southern Cordonbleu) *Uraeginthus angolensis*							
Waxbill, Common *Estrilda astrild*							
Waxbill, Fawn-breasted *Estrilda paludicola*							
Waxbill, Grey (Black-tailed) *Estrilda perreini*							
Waxbill, Orange-breasted (Zebra) *Amandava subflava*							
Waxbill, Violet-eared (Common Grenadier) *Uraeginthus granatinus*							
Weaver, Dark-backed (Forest) *Ploceus bicolor*							
Weaver, Golden (Holub's Golden Weaver) *Ploceus xanthops*							
Weaver, Lesser masked *Ploceus intermedius*							
Weaver, Red-headed *Anaplectes rubriceps*							
Weaver, Southern masked *Ploceus velatus*							
Weaver, Spectacled *Ploceus ocularis*							
Weaver, Thick-billed (Grosbeak) *Amblyospiza albifrons*							
Weaver, Village (Black-headed) *Ploceus cucullatus*							
Wheatear, Capped *Oenanthe pileata*							
Wheatear, Northern (European) *Oenanthe oenanthe*							
White-eye, African yellow *Zosterops senegalensis*							
Whitethroat, Common *Sylvia communis*							
Whydah, Pin-tailed *Vidua macroura*							
Whydah, Shaft-tailed *Vidua regia*							
Widowbird, Fan-tailed (Red-shouldered) *Euplectes axillaris*							
Widowbird, Red-collared *Euplectes ardens*							
Widowbird, White-winged *Eupletes albonotatus*							
Widowbird, Yellow-mantled (Yellow-backed) *Eupletes macroura*							
Wood-Dove, Blue-spotted *Turtur afer*							
Wood-Dove, Emerald-spotted *Turtur chalcospilos*							
Wood-Hoopoe, Green (Red-billed) *Phoeniculus purpureus*							
Wood-Owl, African *Strix woodfordii*							
Woodpecker, Bearded *Dendropicos namaquus*							
Woodpecker, Bennett's *Campethera bennettii*							
Woodpecker, Cardinal *Dendropicos fuscescens*							
Woodpecker, Green-backed (Little-spotted) *Campethera cailliautii*							
Woodpecker, Golden-tailed *Campethera abingoni*							

Woodpecker, Olive *Dendropicos griseocephalus*							
Wren-Warbler, Pale *Calamonastes undosus*							
Wren-Warbler, Stierling's *Calamonastes stierlingi*							

Borassus palms or bottle palms as they are often called, are easily distinguished from the other palm trees by their shape, and are found throughout the Park especially near the Kafue River.

COMMON TREES

African mangosteen *Garcinia livingstonei*	
Baobab *Adansonia digitata*	
Borassus palm *Borassus aethiopum*	
Candelabra tree *Euphorbia ingens*	
Hook thorn Acacia *polyacantha campylacantha*	
Ivory nut palm *Hyphaene (ventricosa) petersiana*	
Jackal-berry *Diospyros mespiliformis.*	
Kafue powder puff *Combretum platypetalum*	
Knob thorn *Acacia nigrescens*	
Leadwood *Combretum imberbe*	
Lowveld albizia *Albizia glaberrima*	
Mane-pod *Dalbergiella nyasae*	
Marula *Sclerocarya (caffra) birrea caffra*	
Mobola plum *Parinari curatellifolia*	
Monkey bread *Piliostigma thonningii*	
Monkey thorn *Acacia galpinii*	
Mopane *Colophospermum mopane*	
Mungongo *(Ricinodendron) or Schinziophyton rautanenii*	
Musikili (Woodland or Natal mahogany) *Trichilia emetica*	
Mutondo (Munondo) *Julbernardia paniculata*	
Phoenix palm (Wild date palm) *Phoenix reclinata*	
Poached egg tree (Bloodwood or Mukwa) *Pterocarpus angolensis*	
Pod mahogany *Afzelia quanzensis*	
Rain tree (Apple-leaf) *Lonchocarpus capassa or Philenoptera violacea*	
Red thorn (Black thorn) *Acacia gerrardii*	
Rubber tree (Horn-pod tree) *Diplorhynchus condylocarpon*	
Sausage tree *Kigelia africana*	
Scotsman's rattle *Amblygonocarpus andongensis*	
Sycamore fig (Cluster fig) *Ficus sycomorus*	
Tree entada *Entada abyssinica*	

Wait-a-bit thorn (Buffalo-thorn) *Ziziphus mucronata*	
Water berry *Syzygium cordatum*	
Water pear *Syzygium guineense barotsense*	
White thorn (Paperbark thorn) *Acacia sieberiana*	
Wild fig *Ficus thonningii (burkei)*	
Wild pear *Dombeya wittei*	
Wild seringa *Burkea africana*	
Winter thorn *Faidherbia albida*	
Wooden banana tree (Mountain mahogany) *Entandrophragma caudatum*	
Yellow wood (Silver cluster-leaf) *Terminalia sericea*	
Zambezi teak *Baikiaea plurijuga*	

The fruits of the sausage tree are unmistakable and can weigh up to 10 kg.

REPTILES

Agama, Black-necked tree *Acanthocerus atricollis*	
Agama, Tropical spiny *Agama armata*	
Boomslang *Dispholidus typus*	
Centipede-eater, Cape *Aparallactus capensis*	
Chameleon, Common flap-necked *Chamaeleo dilepis*	
Cobra, Anchieta's *Naja (Uraeus) anchietae*	
Cobra, Black-necked spitting *Naja (Afronaja) nigricollis*	
Cobra, Forest *Naja (Boulengerina) melanoleuca*	
Cobra, Mozambique spitting *Naja (Afronaja) mossambica*	
Crocodile, Nile *Crocodylus niloticus*	
Egg-eater, Rhombic *Dasypeltis scabra*	
Gecko, Cape dwarf *Lygodactylus capensis*	
Gecko, Chobe dwarf *Lygodactylus chobiensis*	
Gecko, Spotted thick-toed *Pachydactylus punctatus*	
Gecko, Tropical house *Hemidactylus mabouia*	
Lizard, Black-lined plated *Gerrhosaurus nigrolineatus*	
Lizard, Cape rough-scaled *Ichnotropis capensis*	
Lizard, Common rough-scaled *Ichnotropis squamulosa*	
Lizard, Ellenberger's plated *Tetradactylus ellenbergeri*	
Lizard, Ornate scrub *Nucras omata*	
Mamba, Black *Dndroaspis polylepis*	
Monitor, Nile *Varanus niloticus*	
Monitor, Savanna *Varanus albigularis*	
Nightadder, Lined *Causus bilineatus*	
Nightadder, Rhombic *Causus rhombeatus*	
Puffadder *Bitis arietans*	
Python, Southern African *Python natalensis*	
Skink, Anchieta's serpentiform *Eumecia anchietae*	
Skink, Common striped *Trachylepis striata*	
Skink, Gracile limbless *Typhlosaurus gracilis*	

Skink, Spotted-necked snake-eyed *Panaspis maculicollis*	
Skink, Sundevall's writhing *Lygosoma sundevallii*	
Skink, Variable *Trachylepis varia*	
Skink, Wahlberg's snake-eyed *Panaspis wahlbergii*	
Snake, Angolan green *Philothamnus angolensis*	
Snake, Bark *Hemirhagerrhis nototaenia*	
Snake, Bibron's stiletto *Atractaspis bibronii*	
Snake, Brown house *Boaedon capensis*	
Snake, Cape wolf *Lycophidion capense*	
Snake, Dwarf whip *Psammophis angolensis*	
Snake, Eastern tiger *Telescopus semiannulatus*	
Snake, Elongate quill-snouted *Xenocalamus mechowii*	
Snake, Gerard's black & yellow burrowing *Chilorhinophis gerardi*	
Snake, Guenther's garter *Elapsoidea guentheri*	
Snake, Herald *Crotaphopeltis hotamboeia*	
Snake, Katanga worm *Leptotyphlops kafubi*	
Snake, Mole *Pseudaspis cana*	
Snake, Nyasa file *Gonionotophis nyassae*	
Snake, Olive marsh *Natriciteres olivacea*	
Snake, Olive whip *Psammophis phillipsii*	
Snake, Purple-glossed *Amblyodipsas polylepis*	
Snake, Savanna vine *Thelotomis capensis*	
Snake, Schmidt's blind *Afrotyphlops schmidti*	
Snake, Shreve's nocturnal tree *Dipsadoboa shrevei*	
Snake, Semiornate *Meizodon semiomatus*	
Snake, Southeastern green *Philothamnus hoplogaster*	
Snake, Southern file *Gonionotophis capensis*	
Snake, Sooty house *Boaedon fuliginosus*	
Snake, Striped olympic *Psammophis lineatus*	
Snake, Three-lined grass *Psammophylax tritaeniatus*	
Snake, Variegated bush *Philothamnus semivarieagtus*	
Snake, Zambezi garter *Elapsoidea boulengeri*	
Snake, Zambezi giant blind *Megatyphlops mucruso*	

Snake-eater, Eastern *Polemon christyi*	
Terrapin, Helmeted *Pelomedusa rubrufa*	
Terrapin, Okavango hinged *Pelusios bechuanicus*	
Terrapin, Serrated hinged *Pelusios sinuatus*	
Tortoise, Leopard *Stigmochelys pardalis*	
Tortoise, Speke's hinged *Kinixys spekii*	
Viper, Gaboon *Bitis gabonica*	
Worm-lizard, Kafue blunt-headed *Zygaspis kafuensis*	
Worm-lizard, Kalahari blunt-headed *Zygaspis quadrifrons*	
Worm-lizard, Maurice's wedge-snouted *Monopeltis mauricei*	
Worm-lizard, Pestle-tailed *Dalophia pistillum*	

AMPHIBIANS

List provided by D.G.Broadley, Bulawayo, Zimbabwe (2010).

Bullfrog, Tropical African *Pyxicephalus edulis*	
Frog, Anchieta's ridged *Ptychadena anchietae*	
Frog, Angola river *Amietia angolensis*	
Frog, Bocage's burrowing *Leptopelis bocagei*	
Frog, Boettger's dainty *Cacostemum boettgeri*	
Frog, Darling's golden-backed *Hylarana darlingi*	
Frog, Five-striped reed *Hyperolius quinquevittatus*	
Frog, De Witte's spiny reed *Afrixalus wittei*	
Frog, Grassland ridged *Ptychadena porosissima*	
Frog, Guibe's ridged *Ptychadena mosambica*	
Frog, Kafue Flat's reed *Hyperolius marmoratus pyrrhodiction*	
Frog, Kivi reed *Hyperolius kivuensis*	
Frog, Long reed *Hyperolius nasutus*	
Frog, Mababe dwarf puddle *Phrynobatrachus mabebiensis*	
Frog, Mascarene ridged *Ptychadena mascareniensis*	
Frog, Peter's clawed (Plattana) *Xenopus petersii*	
Frog, Power's rain *Breviceps poweri*	

Frog, Small ridged *Ptychadena taenioscelis*	
Frog, Snoring puddle *Phrynobatrachus natalensis*	
Frog, Southern foam-nest *Chiromantis xerampelina*	
Frog, Spotted ridged *Ptychadena subpunctata*	
Frog, Spotted rubber *Phrynomantis affinis*	
Frog, Striped rubber *Phrynomantis bifasciatus*	
Frog, Tremelo sand *Tomoptema cryptotis*	
Frog, Webbed puddle *Phrynobatrachus perpalmatus*	
Frog, Udzungwa ridged *Ptychadena uzungwensis*	
Kassina, Bubbling *Kassina senegalensis*	
Squeaker, Common bush *Arthroleptis stenodactylus*	
Snout-burrower, Barotse *Hemisus barotseensis*	
Snout-burrower, Marbled *Hemisus marmoratus*	
Toad, Beira dwarf *Poyntonophrynus beiranus*	
Toad, Flat-backed *Amietophrynus maculatus*	
Toad, Guttural *Amietophrynus gutturalis*	
Toad, Red *Schismaderma carens*	
Toad, Yellow swamp *Amietophrynus lemairii*	

Mascarene ridged frog found in many of Kafue's grasslands that are flooded in each rainy season.

FISHES OF THE KAFUE RIVER

Barb, Barotse *Barbus barotseensis*	
Barb, Beira *Barbus radiatus*	
Barb, Blackback *Barbus barnardi*	
Barb, Copperstripe *Barbus multilineatus*	
Barb, Dashtail *Barbus poechii*	
Barb, Dwarf *Barbus brevidorsalis*	
Barb, Hyphen *Barbus bifrenatus*	
Barb, Line-spotted *Barbus lineomaculatus*	
Barb, Longbeard *Barbus unitaeniatus*	
Barb, Orangefin *Barbus eutaenia*	
Barb, Red *Barbus fasciolatus*	
Barb, Redspot *Barbus kerstenii*	
Barb, Sickle-fin *Barbus haasianus*	
Barb, Sidespot *Barbus neefi*	
Barb, Spottail *Barbus afrovernayi*	
Barb, Straightfin *Barbus paludinosis*	
Barb, Upjaw *Coptostomabarbus wittei*	
Barb, Zigzag *Barbus miolepis*	
Bottlenose, Western *Mormyrus lacerda*	
Bream, Deepcheek *Sargochromis greenwoodi*	
Bream, Green *Sargochromis codringtoni*	
Bream, Kafue *Sargochromis mortimeri*	
Bream, Pink *Sargochromis giardi*	
Bream, Rainbow *Sargochromis carlottae*	
Bulldog *Marcusenius macrolepidotus*	
Catfish, Blotched *Clarias stappersii*	
Catfish, Blunttooth *Clarias ngamensis*	
Catfish, Sharptooth *Clarias gariepinus*	
Catfish, Silver (Butter Barbel) *Schilbe intermedius*	
Catfish, Smoothhead *Clarius liocephalus*	

Catfish, Snake *Clarias theodorae*	
Catlet, Spotted Sand *Ziareichthys rotundiceps*	
Churchill, Northern *Petrocephalus catostoma*	
Citharine, Broadbar *Nannocharax macropterus*	
Citharine, Multibar *Hemigrammocharax multifasciatus*	
Eel, Longtail Spiny *Aethiomastecembelus frenatus*	
Kapenta *Limnothrissa miodon*	
Kneria, Northern *Kneria polli*	
Killifish, Kafue *Nothobranchius kafuensis*	
Labeo, Redeye *Labeo cylindricus*	
Largemouth, Brownspot *Serranochromis thumbergi*	
Largemouth, Humpback *Serranochromis altus*	
Largemouth, Purpleface *Serranochromis macrocephalus*	
Largemouth, Thinface *Serranochromis augusticeps*	
Mouthbrooder, Southern *Pseuocrenilabrus philander*	
Nembwe (Yellow-belly Bream) *Serranochromis robustus*	
Perch, Blackspot Climbing *Microctenopoma intermedium*	
Perch, Manyspined Climbing *Ctenopoma multispine*	
Pike, African *Hepsetus odoe*	
Robber, Silver *Micralestes acutidens*	
Robber, Slender *Rhabdalestes maunensis*	
Robber, Striped *Brycinus lateralis*	
Squeaker, Largemouth *Synodontis macrostoma*	
Sqeaker, Largespot *Synodontis macrostigma*	
Stonebasher, Dwarf *Pollimyrus castelnaui*	
Suckermouth, Neumann's *Chiloglanis neumanni*	
Tilapia, Banded *Tilapia sparrmanii*	
Tilapia, Greenhead *Oreochromis macrochir*	
Tilapia, Readbreast *Tilapia rendalli*	
Tilapia, Threespot *Oreaochromis andersonii*	
Topminnow, Johnson's *Aplocheilichthys johnstoni*	
Topminnow, Meshscaled *Apolocheilichthys hutereaui*	
Topminnow, Striped *Aplocheilichthys katangae*	

LOCAL NAMES FOR THE MORE COMMON ANIMALS IN LOZI, TONGA, KAONDE, ILA AND BEMBA LANGUAGES

If you go out with a guide, find out which of the five following languages he knows (it is likely to be more than one) and then try using these names when you come across the species listed.

English	Lozi	Tonga	Kaonde	Ila	Bemba
Elephant	Tou	Musovu	Nsovu	Musovu	Nsofu
Hippopotamus	Kubu	Chivubwe	Chovwe	Chivubwe	Mfubu
(Rhinoceros)	Sukulu	Chipembele	Chilangwa	Shempela	Chipembele
Buffalo	Nali	Munyati	Mbowo	Munyati	Mbowo
Zebra	Pizi	Chibize	Chingalika	Chibize	Cholwa
Eland	Pofu	Musefu	Nsefu	Musefu	Nsefu
Kudu	Tolo	Namutentaula	Sontwa	Namutentaula	Ntandala
Sable	Fumbokaloko	Lwengu	Mfumbo	Kantunta; Kafumbwi	Kanshiliye
Roan	Kwlatayeseta; Kwalatasweu	Chilumbu lumbu	Ntengu	Chilumbu lumbu	Mpelembe
Wildebeest	Kokon'u	Munyumbwe	Chimfulwe	Munyumbwe	Nyumbu
Hartebeest	Kakatombwi	Katombwi	Nkonzhi	Konzi	Inkonshi
Waterbuck	Ngunduma	Mukulu	Mukambi	Mukulu	Chuswe
Reedbuck	Kaputi	Naluvwi	Kasha	Naluvwi	Imfwi
Impala	Luondo	Lubondwe	Lupala	Nanzeli; Shashubila	Impala
Puku	Mutinya	Hichisusu	Nsebula	Sichisunu	Nsebula
Oribi	Kamunda	Nakafwifwi	Kapunda	Nacindwe	Sele
Lechwe	Lizwi	Nanja	Honge	Nanja	Inja
Bushbuck	Mbabala	Mbabala	Ngulungu	Sichibawala; Sichibange	Chisongo
Sitatunga	Sitatunga	Sichiobe	Mbuji	Sichinzobe	Nsobe
Common duiker	Kaputi	Nakasha	Kasha	Nakasha	Mpombo
Blue duiker	Kasenda	Kabuluku	Kantimba		
Yellow-backed duiker		Chikunji			Chinkundiya-mateshi
Grysbok	Katimba	Timba	Chingomba	Timba	Katili
Klipspringer		Sense, Njelele, Kanganam-tengere	Kakoko Mabwe		Chibushi-mabwe
Steenbok	Kabanyane	Kabu, Kabo, Tukaula			
Warthog	Njili	Munjile	Mpenge	Shankole	Njili
Bushpig	Kulube	Inkulube	Ngulube	Nkuntula	Kapoli
Lion	Tau	Shumbwa	Bokwe	Shumbwa	Nkalamo

English	Lozi	Tonga	Kaonde	Ila	Bemba
Leopard	Ingwe	Shiluwe	Chisumpa	Shiluwe	Mbwili
Cheetah	Linau	Malama	Chinkoman-koma, Mpumpunta	Malama	Chiseketa
Wild Dog	Liakanyani	Umpe	Musuka	Musaka, Umpa	Mumbulu
Hyaena	Sitongwani	Suntwe	Mungolwe	Kabwenga	Chimbwi
Baboon			Mpombo		Kolwe ya mpali
Vervet monkey	Njoko	Cheta, Sokwi	Kolwe	Sokwe	Kolwe wa ncheta
Porcupine	Sinuku	Inungu	Nungu	Chminungwe	Chinungi

COMMON TREES IN THE KAFUE NATIONAL PARK

African mangosteen *Garcinia livingstonei*
This is one of the most delectable of the African wild fruits, ripening in October-November. It grows only on river banks and near Mukambi and it is easily identified by its long upright branches that distinguish it clearly from other riverine trees.

Baobab *Adansonia digitata*
Large baobabs occur on the road to Mumbwa from Lusaka and at Mukambi Safari Lodge, Treetops Schools' Camp, around Nanzhila and elsewhere.

Borassus palm *Borassus aethiopum*
Distinguished from the Hyphaene palm by its sturdy erect habit and the unusual bottle-like swelling of the trunk. The large, edible, sweet smelling fruits contain three nuts that ripen late in the year and are relished by elephants. The Hyphaene has a single nut. The palm swift attaches its nest to the lower leaves.

Candelabrum tree *Euphorbia ingens*
Commonly found on termite mounds. The juicy fruits are dispersed by hornbills, and other frugivorous birds. Surprisingly, black rhino are particularly attracted to the latex, which is toxic to nearly all other species and is used as a poison to kill fish.

Hook thorn *Acacia polyacantha campylacantha*
The presence of this tree in quantity usually indicates old cultivation or a village

site on good soil. The crushed roots have a pungent smell and are said to be repellent to reptiles and to keep snakes out of a house or crocodiles from a river crossing. Kudu and eland eat the foliage. The roots are also used to treat snakebite.

Ivory nut palm *Hyphaene (ventricosa) petersiana*
This palm is more slender and less rigid than Borassus. The crown is sometimes cut out and tapped for palm wine. In some places over-exploitation for palm wine, combined with annual burning, is eliminating the species locally. Elephants are fond of the nuts and dislodge them by pressing the underside of the base of their trunk against the tree and shaking it vigorously. Dickinson's kestrel usually breeds in these palms and its distribution is governed by movement by the elephant population and buried by dung beetles. Palm swifts also nest in this tree.

Jackal-berry *Diospyros mespiliformis.*
This tree grows usually on river banks and on termite mounds near pools. Parrots, green pigeons and other birds, as well as bushbabies, monkeys, civets, jackals and elephant eat its fruit. It is a favourite nesting tree for the fish-eagle. Its wood used to be valued for wagons and wagon gear, cabinet making and canoes.

Kafue powder puff *Combretum platypetalum*
Normally an inconspicuous low shrub. This suffrutex (a group of woody plants that are highly resistant to fire) has a stout woody rootstock and underground stem, and is covered with brilliant crimson bloom in the middle of the dry season stimulated by the passage of fire. It is widespread as an indicator of repeated burning and is very common in large areas in the central and southern parts of the Park, such as Katinti.

Knob thorn *Acacia nigrescens*
This medium-sized, thorny tree is commonly found in open woodland and on termitaria. The knobs on the trunk result from the growth of bark at the site of the original thorns at the base of the leaves. It flowers in early spring producing much sweet-scented nectar. Kudu are fond of its pods and foliage, especially of trees knocked down by elephants. It is a favourite nesting tree of the sparrow weaver whose nests are often on the western side of the tree. The tree is exceptionally fire-resistant and the timber is resistant to termites and has been widely used for mine props

Leadwood *Combretum imberbe*
The timber is excessively hard and heavy and has been used to make hoe blades. The ash is very fine and white and said to contain a high lime content. It has been used as a substitute for whitewash.

Lowfeld Albizia *Albizia glaberrima*
A large tree growing on the banks of the Kafue River. A tree at Kafwala Wildlife Camp is probably a hybrid between this species and *A. harveyi*.

Mane-pod *Dalbergiella nyasae*
The most common small tree in the Park and one of the first of the woodland trees to flower.

Marula *Sclerocarya (caffra) birrea caffra*
There is a large specimen of this tree near the old Ngoma Lodge viewing tower. The wood is soft and not at all durable but it is used extensively for carving stools, dishes and drums. The fruits are edible and used for distilling alcoholic drinks. The fruits are also a favourite food of elephant and kudu, the latter spitting out the pips during rumination.

Mobola plum *Parinari curatellifolia*
This is an evergreen tree that produces plum-like fruits, which are eaten by fruit-bats and elephants. When kudu or eland eat them, the fruits are swallowed whole but the pips are spat out during rumination. The roots are sometimes used in the preparation of both ear drops and eye drops.

Monkey bread *Piliostigma thonningii*
The big thick pods are eaten by many browsing animals. Soap can be made from the unripe pods and a medicine for coughs from the roots.

Monkey thorn *Acacia galpinii*
One of the largest of the Acacias, growing on deep alluvial soils or on termite mounds. Prolific flowering occurs on the leafless tree in August; the flowers are pale yellow borne on purple inflorescences.

Mopane *Colophospermum mopane*
A tree that is well-represented on the clay soil areas along the Nanzhila River and south of Nanzhila Plains Safari Lodge. It is also found in areas degraded by fire in the central area north of the Musa River and in small patches near Moshi.

Mungongo *(Ricinodendron) or Schinziophyton rautanenii*
This deciduous tree bears leaves during the rainy season and has stark upward pointing branches in the dry season. Its almond-like fruits are eaten by elephants, porcupines and parrots. The wood is brittle and very light and is similar in some respects to balsa and oil from the seed kernel is used for making high quality soap.

Musikili (Woodland or Natal mahogany) *Trichilia emetica*
A large, evergreen tree with a dense, rounded crown, known best for its three-lobed, velvety fruits that contain glossy, black seeds partly covered by a bright, scarlet coat (aril). It is found in undisturbed riparian woodland. There are some fine specimens in the south at Mubi Pool, near Nanzhila Plains Safari Camp.

Mutondo (Munondo) *Julbernardia paniculata*
Probably the most abundant large tree in the Park. It is a major honey source as it flowers after the rains when there is little else. The bark of dead trees burns with a bright flame, useful for temporary lighting

Phoenix palm (Wild date palm) *Phoenix reclinata*
Grows along edges of rivers and streams. Found at many places along the Kafue River above Itezhi-Tezhi. The numerous pale yellow flowers form exceptionally beautiful downward curving "sprays", which are originally enclosed in long, tapering outer sheaths or "bracts".

Poached egg tree (Bloodwood or Mukwa) *Pterocarpus angolensis*
This is one of the most valuable timber trees of Zambia, being easy to work and suitable for almost all purposes, and the roots, flowers, bark and red sap are widely used in traditional medicine. It is leafless for a very long period of the dry season. It is easily identified by its rough bark and large, round seed pods, which have a raised prickly centre. The bark is frequently stripped and eaten by elephant. It is being selectively logged in many places these days.

Pod mahogany *Afzelia quanzensis*
The heavy woody pods contain bright black and orange seeds, which are used for ornaments. The red arils attached to the seed are eaten by hornbills distributing them in the process; rodents eat the seeds. It blooms in October and the fallen flowers are eaten by impala and bushbuck. The timber is good for furniture and is sometimes used for making canoes. An infusion of the roots is said to be a cure for bilharzia and is usually injected into the bladder through a thin hollow grass stem.

Rain tree (Apple-leaf) *Lonchocarpus capassa or Philenoptera violacea*
Often late in the dry season, large colonies of the nymphs of a large froghopper congregate on the branches and their intense feeding activity causes a drip, which can create small puddles beneath the tree. Foliage and flowers are eaten by kudu and eland in the spring and apparently have high food value. This is regarded by some people as a lucky tree, a leaf decoction being given by traditional doctors to disputants in an argument.

Red thorn (Black thorn) *Acacia gerrardii*
Usually a small tree, often stunted, on clay termite mounds or on black cotton soil, such as the wide savanna north of Chunga that was once a favourite habitat of rhino.

Rubber tree (Horn-pod tree) *Diplorhynchus condylocarpon*
This tree is browsed by many herbivores and is one of the favourite foods of elephant, which frequently knock them down to eat the leaves. Latex collected from the unripe fruits and from the stem is used in the preparation of birdlime and the leaves are used in making game calls, or "chinyenye" as it is called in the Bemba language.

Sausage tree *Kigelia africana*
The large red flowers open in the evening and are pollinated by sunbirds and possibly also by bats. The fallen flowers are eaten by kudu and bushbuck. The long fibrous fruits are occasionally eaten by baboons and elephant, but rhino are particularly fond of them. Some African tribes add pieces of the fruit to brewing beer in order to aid fermentation. The powdered fruit is sometimes used as a cure for ulcers

Scotsman's rattle *Amblygonocarpus andongensis*
A large tree on sandy soils. The dark brown woody pods, square in cross-section, with seeds that rattle when the pod is shaken, are unmistakable. The mature fruits fall to the ground for elephant and other herbivores to consume and disperse the seeds.

Sycamore fig (Cluster fig) *Ficus sycamorus*
This fig tree also produces a valuable crop of fruit. The fruit is larger than that of *F. burkei*. Not only are they eaten by birds and fruit bats, but impala will conspicuously visit the trees to feed on the fallen fruits as they do at Chunga camp. The Chaplin's barbet is strongly associated with old specimens of this tree. The trampling of grasses nearby adds to its protection from fire.

Tree entada *Entada abyssinica*
This tree has very curious pods and is said to be used in rain making ceremonies in some countries. It appears to be especially favoured by buffalo for scratching and hence one local name, Chikumbamboo, meaning "Buffalo Hide".

Wait-a-bit thorn (Buffalo-thorn) *Ziziphus mucronata*
The straight and hooked thorns serve to distinguish this tree. The fruits are eaten by a variety of birds, particularly the go-away-bird and by monkeys. Another member of this genus is the tree that, according to tradition, provided the crown of thorns suffered by Jesus Christ upon the Cross.

Water berry *Syzygium cordatum*
The presence of this tree always indicates the proximity of permanent water as it commonly grows on riverbanks near springs and the margins of dambos. Leaf has virtually no stalk. The fruits are eaten by many birds, particularly green pigeons.

Water pear *Syzygium guineense barotsense*
This tree differs from *S. cordatum* by the presence of a leaf stalk and a generally more greyish-white colour. It grows typically on riverbanks, with its branches leaning right out over the water. Green pigeons and trumpeter hornbills feed on its fruits that become a dark pinkish colour when mature. The fruits also float and are dispersed by floodwaters in the early rains. Elephant browse the foliage during the dry season.

White thorn (Paperbark thorn) *Acacia sieberiana*
This tree encroaches into grasslands as a result of too frequent bush fires. In the spring pods, and foliage are eaten by impala and elephants; the latter are evidently causing a lot of damage to this species all over the Nanzhila Plains, where many of the trees are broken down exposing the yellow-white heartwood

Wild fig *Ficus thonningii (burkei)*
This fig tree produces abundant tiny fruits eaten by many birds. The grove at old Ngoma Lodge supports many small fruit-eating bats and fruit-eating birds.

Wild pear *Dombeya wittei*
A much-branched shrub almost confined to the Kafue River system, although also in Katanga. Sweetly scented clusters of pink flowers appear from June-August.

Wild seringa *Burkea africana*
A very fire-resistant species yielding a hard and heavy timber used for rough work and for parquet flooring. Powdered bark and pods are used as fish poison. Kudu eat the foliage in the spring.

Winter thorn *Faidherbia albida*
This large tree is leafless until the end of the rains and remains in leaf throughout the dry season. It usually indicates good soil suitable for dry season cultivation and it is often a pioneer species on alluvial soils. It fruits from September onwards and the pods are eaten by elephant, eland, kudu and impala. The timber is used for dugout canoes and the bark for a medicine for diarrhoea and for stupefying fish. It is a sacred tree of the BaTwa people.

Wooden banana tree (Mountain mahogany) *Entandrophragma caudatum*
A large, fire-sensitive tree when young, which may account for its being largely restricted to thickets where bush fires seldom penetrate. The Barotse Royal barge is made of this timber, which is also valuable for furniture. Leather tanned with the bark is very hard and is used for drums. Large specimens grow in the Musa thicket between Ngoma and Itezhi-Tezhi/Musa River.

Yellow wood (Silver cluster-leaf) *Terminalia sericea*
This tree is a pioneer species that is very fire-resistant and invades the teak forests when they have been damaged by fire, as can be seen very clearly today along the edges of the Ngoma Forest. There is also a remarkably uniform stand all round the north side of old Ngoma Lodge, where the species now occupies land that was once open grass. The timber is yellow and is very tough and insect resistant. It is especially good for use as beams and lintels. Wild animals hardly use this at all, although the bark is eaten by elephants.

Zambezi teak *Baikiaea plurijuga*
This is a very valuable timber tree forming forests on the Zambezi sands. It is very fire susceptible and owes its survival to the existence of large herds of heavy grazing animals, which feed on and trample out the inflammable grasses, considerably reducing the fire hazard. The general welfare of the forest is dependent on the presence of these animals. It blooms from December until May, the flowers being pollinated by sunbirds. The timber is very hard and heavy and is amongst the world's best for parquet flooring. It is resistant to termites and therefore used for railway sleepers.

LOCAL NAMES OF THE MORE COMMON TREES IN LOZI, TONGA & KAONDE LANGUAGES

English	Lozi	Tonga	Kaonde
African mangosteen	Mukwanga	Mukwananga	
Borassus palm	Mukulwani	Mapokwe	Kampungu
Hook thorn	Mukotokoto	Mumbu	Mukoka
Ivory nut palm	Munganda	Mapokwe	Kambili
Jackal-berry	Muchenja	Muchenja	Mukyengya
Kafue powder puff	Kachingamwezi		
Knob thorn	Mukwenya	Mwaba	Muzalazambe
Leadwood	Muzwili	Mubimba	
Marula	Mulula	Muongo	Muongo
Mobola	Mubula	Mula	Mupundu
Monkey bead	Musekese	Musekese	Kifumbe
Mungongo	Mungongo	Ndubalala	
Phoenix palm	Nzalu	Kisonga	
Poached egg tree	Mukwa	Mukula	Mukulakula
Pod mahogany	Mwande	Mupapa	Musambamfwa
Rain tree	Mupanda	Mukololo	
Rubber tree	Mulya	Mutowa	Mwenge
Sausage tree	Muzungula	Muzungula	Kifungula
Sycamore fig	Mukuyu	Mukuyu	Mukuyu
Tree entada	Mukumbwangombe		
Wait-a-bit thorn	Mukalu	Mwichechete	Kankona
Water berry	Mutoya	Katope	Musombo
Water pear	Katope	Musombo	
White thorn	Mutubatuba	Mumpangala	Mwiba
Wild fig	Muminamboma/Mutata	-	
Wild seringa	Museshe	Museshe	Kapanga
Winter-thorn	Munga	Musangu	Mwiba
Wooden banana tree	Mupumewa	Mupingili	
Yellow wood	Muhonono	Mutwamaila	
Zambezi teak	Mukushi		

INDEX

Access 9, 20, 39, 49, 54, 55, 56, 57, 58, 67, 69, 83, 93, 94, 95, 104, 113, 118
Accommodation 7, 59, 67, 74, 78, 81, 88, 101, 112
Airstrip 51, 52, 56, 58, 74, 78, 87, 92, 102, 104
Amphibians 41, 105,128, 142, 172
Annual burning 8, 18, 19, 128, 178
Antelope 3, 21, 23, 24, 25, 26, 27, 28, 29, 30, 31, 33, 46,110, 122, 126, 128
Area Warden's office at Chunga 95, 123, 124, 133
Baikiaea 18, 19, 169, 183
Banking and currency 138
Barbel (catfish) 42, 50, 51, 81, 85, 107, 138, 174
Barotseland 6
Bernard Calonne 104
Bilharzia 42, 43, 133, 180
Bilili Springs 105
Biodiversity 118, 119, 120, 126, 128, 130
Birds 3, 17, 20, 21, 38, 39, 41, 48, 49, 50, 74, 85, 90, 93, 96, 100, 101, 103, 105, 107, 108, 111, 115, 126, 127, 128, 141, 142,143, 144, 151, 177, 178, 179, 180, 181, 182, 183
Black barbel (catfish) 42, 51, 107
Black-cheeked lovebird 3, 21, 38, 111, 115, 159
Black rhino 21. 22, 85, 176, 177, 181
Blue duiker 3, 22, 30, 73, 80, 108, 128, 145, 176
Boating 5, 53, 70, 73, 74, 80, 81, 83, 91, 97, 109
Bookings, enquiries and useful contacts 59, 139
Borassus palm 20, 167, 168, 177, 178, 184
Botswana 35, 129
Bream 50, 51, 81, 138, 174, 175
Buffalo 3, 19, 24, 32, 70, 79, 80, 86, 90, 94, 96, 108, 110, 122, 128, 135, 145, 176, 181
Busanga Airstrip at Masozhi 92
Busanga Plain 5, 8, 9, 12, 16, 19, 20, 22, 23, 24, 25, 26, 27, 28, 29, 32, 40, 55, 83, 85, 87, 89, 90, 91, 92, 93, 94, 110, 123, 128
Bush Camp 59, 61, 136
Bushbaby 36, 123
Bushbuck 22, 28, 85, 96, 122, 145, 176, 180, 181
Business Centre 123, 124
Camping 51, 53, 59, 63, 71, 72, 76, 77, 79, 81, 83, 97, 100, 101, 102, 103, 104, 112, 113, 114, 115, 136, 137
Camps 3, 7, 41, 49, 51, 54, 57, 59, 63, 64, 68, 69, 80, 84, 85, 89, 98, 106, 107, 120, 124, 134, 136
Campsite 50, 59, 61, 79, 81, 85, 100, 137
Canoeing 53, 96, 97, 104
Car rental 137, 141
Cattle 6, 9, 10, 54, 80
Central African Plateau 3, 5
Central Area 4, 5, 12, 37, 56, 66, 88, 94, 95, 96, 97, 98, 99, 107123, 124, 178, 179
Chacma baboon 123, 145
Chalanta Entrance Gate 56, 69
Chaplin's barbet 21, 38, 85, 93, 151, 181
Charges 52, 53, 60
Cheetah 21, 31, 33, 34, 50, 90, 94, 96, 108, 110, 128, 145, 177
Chibemba Plain 86, 88
Chief Kaingu 8, 97
Chief Musungwa's Palace 56
Chunga, Northern Area, HQ 7, 12, 19, 24, 26, 27, 51, 58, 95, 97, 101, 105, 123,
124, 127, 129, 133, 134, 181
Civet 36, 145, 178
Climate 13, 15, 22, 43, 46, 118, 128, 129
Clinics 134, 136
Common duiker 22, 29, 31, 145, 176
Conservation 3, 6, 43, 49, 50, 118, 123, 124, 128, 129, 130
Control and management of fire 10, 127, 129
Copperbelt 52, 54, 112
Cordon Controlled Area 6
Cordon Road 54, 55, 56, 115
Crested guineafowl 3, 39, 108, 156
Crocodile 19, 39, 40, 73, 85, 107, 122, 133, 135, 170, 178
Cultural visits to local villages 77, 97, 109
Dambo 5, 15, 16, 24, 25, 33, 39, 70, 73, 80, 122, 182
Darrell Watt 80
Director General, Zambia Wildlife Authority 58, 139, 140
Diseases 34, 119
Distances 24, 35, 55, 86, 136
Driving after dark 66, 133
Dry season 4, 15, 16, 17, 23, 26, 27, 42, 44, 46, 48, 55, 57, 73, 76, 89, 90, 91, 105, 110, 115, 125 126, 178, 179, 180, 182
Dundumwezi Entrance Gate 5, 18, 24, 31, 52, 53, 54, 55, 105, 115, 123, 137
Early burning 19, 125, 127
Ecological separation 122
Ecology 8, 9, 10, 41, 90, 125
Ecosystem 8, 10, 22, 43, 118, 121, 122
Eland 19, 22, 24, 25, 86, 96, 122, 127, 128, 144, 145, 176, 178, 179, 180, 182
Elephant 3, 19, 21, 23, 35, 50, 73, 85, 86, 97, 110, 115, 120, 121, 122, 127, 128, 135, 145, 176, 177, 178, 179, 180, 181, 182, 183
Elephant Orphanage Project 52, 107, 108
Entrance gates 49, 52
Entry permits 132, 139
Family rooms 74, 88, 99, 102, 103, 112, 113
Fauna 5, 42, 43, 123, 128, 133
Filling stations 54, 56, 57, 69, 137
Fire and firebreaks 120,124, 127
Fish 8, 9, 10, 21, 38, 39, 41 42, 50, 51, 52, 71, 105, 107, 123, 128, 142, 174, 175, 177, 182
Fishing 5, 8, 9, 20, 41, 49, 50, 51, 52, 55, 66, 70, 71, 73, 74, 75, 78, 80, 81, 83, 85, 90, 91, 97, 105, 109, 112, 129, 133, 138
Fishing and picnic spots/sites 50, 51, 52, 55, 66, 133
Fishing competition 112
Fishing tackle 50,138
Flagship species 49, 50, 128
Floodplains 3, 4, 5, 12, 15, 16, 22, 24, 27, 28, 58, 80, 93, 101, 102, 116
Fly Camp 59. 79
Food and equipment 136
Forest 3, 4, 5, 8, 10, 18, 30, 32, 39, 40, 108, 125, 128, 129, 183

Frank Arsell 6
Fuel 54, 57, 136, 137
Gaboon viper 18, 40, 172
Game Management Areas (GMA) 2, 7, 8, 23, 38, 49, 62, 63, 70, 77, 78, 95, 99, 100, 101, 105, 108, 119, 123, 124, 128, 129, 151
Geology 4, 10, 11, 12, 13, 49
Giant stick insect 18
Giraffe 22, 122, 127
Grysbok 22, 30, 108, 145, 176
Habitat management 128
Health and safety 134, 135
Hippo Mine 67, 69, 73, 74
Hippo Mine-Mushingashi-Lubungu Area 67, 69, 73
Hippopotamus 3, 16, 19, 21, 23, 73, 85, 107, 122, 123, 135, 146, 176
History 5, 8, 12, 73, 105, 109
Honey badger 36, 146
Hook Bridge Entrance Gate 57, 70, 83
Hospital 134, 136
Hot springs 10, 75, 77, 80, 86
Hubs 63, 74, 99, 112
Human Wildlife Conflicts 130
Hunting 6, 7, 8, 10, 22, 24, 27, 40, 105, 108, 124
Hyphaene palm 20, 168, 177, 178
Hyrax (Dassie) 35, 97, 112, 146
Ila 6, 9, 10. 97, 109, 112, 176, 177
Impala 18, 22, 27, 33, 70, 85, 96, 115, 122, 126, 146, 176,180, 181, 182
Important Bird Areas 3, 17, 38, 142
Invertebrates 42, 43, 105, 126, 128
Itezhi-Tezhi Dam 6, 7, 12, 55, 105, 107, 110, 111, 113, 120, 134
Itezhi-Tezhi road D769 53, 95, 105, 112, 113
Jackal 33, 34, 90, 146, 178
Julbernardia 16, 168, 180
Kabanga Entrance Gate 54, 55, 83
Kabulushi Gate 4, 57, 69
Kafue Flats 6, 10, 21, 56, 109, 116
Kafue Hook 8, 12
Kafue Hook Bridge 18, 57, 67, 69, 70, 83, 85, 93, 94, 95, 100, 123
Kafue River 3, 4, 6, 12, 18, 20, 23, 26, 27, 28, 37, 39, 40, 41, 50, 51, 55, 58, 67, 70, 74, 76, 77, 79, 80, 81, 82, 83, 85, 86, 88, 95, 96, 99, 101, 102, 103, 104, 105, 109, 110, 123, 129, 167, 174, 179, 180,182
Kafue River Café 88
Kafue Trust 3, 60, 141, 144
Kafwala Rapids 85, 86
Kaindabaila Hill 5, 12, 95, 97
Kalala 7
Kalenje 13, 18, 52
Kalomo (District) 6, 53, 54, 55, 137
Kaonde 10, 176, 177, 184
Kasempa 6, 8, 48, 53, 54, 55, 56, 57, 69, 129
Kasempa road D181 53, 57, 69
Kasha River 23, 110
Kasungula 54
Kaunga 25, 52
Kavango-Zambezi Transfrontier Conservation Area KAZA-TFCA 23, 129
Klipspringer 22, 31, 128, 146, 176
KNP rules and regulations 133
Kondakamwale 51, 63, 89
KPOA 66, 141
Kudu 18, 22, 25, 96, 108, 122, 128, 146, 176, 178, 179, 180, 181, 182
Laboratory and herbarium 129
La Hacienda Hotel 67
Lake Itezhi-Tezhi 5, 6, 7, 24, 27, 31, 32, 40, 42, 46, 49, 50, 51, 52, 56, 95, 97, 105, 107, 108, 109, 111, 112, 113, 114, 123
Lakeside Drive 114
Late fires 18, 125, 127
Len Vaughan 5
Leopard 3, 31, 33, 73, 80, 86, 90, 94, 96, 108, 122, 128, 135, 146, 177
Lichtenstein's hartebeest 3, 16, 22, 26, 32, 70, 73, 80, 85, 93, 96, 108, 122, 126, 128, 146, 176
Lion 3, 21, 24, 31, 32, 33, 34, 35, 73, 78, 79, 80, 85, 90, 94, 96, 108, 110, 122, 128, 135, 146, 176
Livingstone 52, 54, 55, 57, 92, 102, 104, 110, 112, 137, 138, 139, 140, 141
Local communities 8, 9, 10, 49, 124, 127, 128, 130
Local names for the more common animals in Lozi, Tonga, Kaonde, Ila and Bemba languages 176
Local names of the more common trees 184
Lodges and Camps 3, 41, 57, 61, 62, 63, 64, 124, 134, 136
Lubalanzuki Hill 5, 12, 95, 97
Lufupa 7, 23, 26, 28, 33, 40, 51, 58, 83, 85, 86, 88, 89, 90, 123
Lunga River 4, 58, 69, 78, 123
Lusaka 52, 54, 55, 56, 67, 83, 89, 92, 95, 102, 112, 132, 137, 138, 139, 140, 141, 142, 177
Lushimba 7, 51, 58
M9 Highway 54, 55, 56, 57, 66, 67, 83, 85, 95, 96, 100, 105, 113, 123, 137
Mammals 3, 6, 18, 20, 21, 22, 23, 31, 34, 36, 38, 48, 49, 73, 80, 121, 122, 126, 127, 142, 144, 145, 148
Management of traditional fishing 9, 90, 129
Management Zones of the KNP 123
Managing the Kafue National Park 118
Maps 4, 49, 83, 136, 137
Masozhi Gate 55, 92
Mayukweyukwe Area 51, 67, 69, 70
Miombo 5, 16, 17, 18, 19, 25, 26, 29, 30, 31, 43, 70, 73, 80, 96, 97, 102, 107, 125, 126, 127
Mongoose 36, 37, 146
Mongu 52, 54, 55, 56
Monitor 39, 40,107, 122, 128, 170
Monze 55, 57
Mopane 5, 13, 17, 18, 19, 25, 67, 110, 126, 128, 168, 179
Moshi 7, 26, 51, 85, 89, 179
Mufunta GMA 95, 96
Mulanga ZAWA Entrance Gate 57
Mulobezi 31, 54, 55, 57, 105, 111
Mumbwa 53, 54, 55, 56, 57, 67, 69, 70, 71, 95, 99, 100, 101, 105, 123, 137, 139, 140, 177
Mumbwa Game Management Area 70, 95, 99, 100, 101, 105
Munga 127, 184
Mungosiya River 18
Musa Entrance Gate 56, 57, 112
Musa River 5, 6, 8, 12, 19, 31, 52, 107, 123, 179, 183
Mushingashi Conservancy 30, 53, 56, 57, 67, 69, 73, 79, 80, 81
Mushingashi River 69
Mutumbwe Hill 4
Mweengwa checkpoint 95
Mwengwa Rapids 5
Nakalomwe Entrance Gate 56
Nakalomwe Hill 109
Nalusanga Entrance Gate 53, 54, 55, 66, 67, 70, 95, 123, 137
Namibia 129
Namitwi Loop 108
Namwala 55, 56, 57, 95, 105, 108, 109, 129
Namwala GMA 95, 105
Nangandwe Pool 23, 115
Nanzhila 5, 7, 8, 9, 15, 16, 21, 23, 25, 26, 27, 35, 41, 52, 56, 57, 58, 59, 110, 111, 115, 116, 123, 129, 177, 179, 180, 182
Nanzhila Plains 5, 16, 23, 25, 58,

110, 111, 182
Nanzhila River 9, 15, 115, 116, 179
National Parks 3, 35, 43, 118, 123, 129, 133
Ndulumina 7
Ngoma 7, 18, 19, 23, 24, 26, 30, 39, 40, 52, 56, 57, 58, 105, 107, 108, 109, 114, 123, 124, 128, 129, 134, 179, 182, 183
Ngoma aerodrome 56, 57, 58
Night drives 33, 35, 36, 60, 66, 137
Nkala River 12, 23, 25, 26, 52, 123
Nocturnal species 30, 32, 33, 34, 35, 36, 37
North-East 4, 24, 25, 30, 48, 56, 66, 67, 68, 69, 74, 77, 78, 123
North-West 4, 5, 30, 44, 66, 83, 84, 85, 93, 123
Northern Rhodesia 5, 142
Ntemwa 51, 83, 85, 89, 90
Old Nkala Fort 109
Old Nkala Mission 108
Open Africa 49, 50, 141
Oribi 16, 19, 22, 28, 93, 108, 146, 176
Otters 37, 85, 107, 122, 146
Pangolin 36, 146
Park boundary 3, 6, 8, 12, 16, 18, 26, 30, 51, 52, 54, 77, 79, 82, 96, 107, 108, 120, 123
Park fees 52, 53, 60
Park regulations 5, 52, 133
Phoenix Palm 20, 100, 168, 180, 184
Photographers 48, 49
Piamanzi hot springs 80
Picnic 49, 50, 51, 52, 55, 66, 133
Pike 50, 51, 81, 138, 175
Plains Road 115
Poaching 3, 8, 22, 28, 107, 120, 121, 125
Porcupine 35, 146, 177, 179
Price bands 59, 60
Provincial Administration 6, 8
Puku 6, 7, 22, 27, 33, 70, 80, 85, 90, 93, 95, 96, 110, 122, 142, 146, 176
Radio communications 136
Rainfall 2, 44, 46
Rainy season 9, 46, 48, 49, 56, 108, 173, 179
Red lechwe 3, 19, 22, 27, 28, 56, 90, 93, 110, 120, 122, 128, 146, 176
Reedbuck 16, 18, 19, 22, 27, 33, 70, 73, 80, 96, 108, 146, 176
Regional Manager, ZAWA Western Region, Mumbwa 123, 139, 140
Reptiles 39, 41, 128, 142, 170, 178
Rescue assistance 134, 136
Research and monitoring 41, 73, 121, 123, 128, 139
Riparian woodland 5, 20, 39, 72, 73, 77, 80, 85, 90, 114, 126, 128, 180
Riverine grassland 15, 16
Roads 2, 3, 9, 49, 52, 53, 54, 66, 67, 68, 83, 84, 89, 95, 96, 98, 106, 107, 118, 120, 124, 133
Roan antelope 3, 16, 18, 19, 21, 22, 25, 26, 73, 80, 85, 86, 90, 93, 96, 108, 126, 128, 144, 146, 176
Rock hyrax 35, 97, 112, 146
Rules to remember 6, 132, 133, 134, 135
Sable antelope 3, 16, 19, 21, 22, 25, 26, 50, 70, 73, 80, 85, 86, 96, 97, 108, 122, 126, 127, 128, 146, 176
Savanna 3, 15, 19, 25, 40, 121, 181
Seasonality 46, 83
Self-drive 49, 50, 53, 71, 72, 74, 79, 83, 85, 137
Shakalongo Plain 25, 110
Shibatwa hills 31, 107
Simungoma 54, 55, 57
Sitatunga 19, 22, 29, 73, 80, 90, 128, 147, 176
Slaty egret 3, 21, 155
Soils 10, 12, 13, 17, 18, 19, 31, 35, 66, 108, 110, 126, 141, 179, 181, 182
Southern African Development Community (SADC) 52, 130, 132
Southern Area HQ Ngoma 57, 123, 124
Southern part of KNP 4, 6, 12, 13, 31, 37, 40, 52, 57, 66, 83, 85, 97, 99, 105, 106, 108, 109, 110, 112, 113, 123, 178
Southern part of the North-West Area 83, 85
Speed limits 66, 133
Spinal Road 31, 40, 52, 57, 83, 85, 95, 105, 107
Spotting checklist 23, 144
Springhare 35, 147
Steenbok 22, 31, 147
Suffrutex savanna 19, 178
Swamp 10, 19, 20, 29, 89, 90, 128
T1 Highway 54, 55, 137
Tateyoyo gate 53, 55, 56, 66, 83
Teak forest 5, 18, 30, 39, 108, 126, 128, 169, 183, 184
Termitaria 17, 25, 43, 110, 178
Thicket 5, 18, 24, 25, 28, 30, 33, 39, 40, 73, 80, 86, 108, 110, 122, 183
Tilapia 21, 50, 175
Tonga 10, 112, 176, 177, 184
Tourism 8, 9, 10, 24, 42, 49, 58, 66, 83, 99, 107, 120, 124, 130, 139, 14
Tracks 21, 28, 35, 49, 80, 83, 114
Traditional fishing 9, 129
Travel Tips 132
Treetops Schools' Camp 7, 38, 51, 8
85, 89, 177
Tsessebe 22
Tsetse 6, 10, 42, 134
Twin Baobab trees 54, 67
Uncontrolled burning 38, 103, 120, 124, 125, 126, 128
Usufruct Rights 8, 129
Vegetation 8, 15, 17, 19, 20, 21, 29, 32, 35, 43, 49, 58, 72, 77, 85, 104, 107, 114, 120, 122, 126, 127, 128
Visas 132
Vital equipment for 4 x 4 journeys 13
Walking 60, 70, 73, 79, 81, 83, 91, 97, 104, 109, 133, 136
Warthog 18, 31, 32, 70, 74, 85, 122
147, 176
Waterbuck 16, 19, 22, 26, 58, 108, 115, 122, 128, 147, 176
Wattled crane 3, 21, 74, 111, 153
Waypoints 57, 59, 62, 64, 66, 137
Western Province 6, 108, 135
Western Boundary 3, 6, 12, 16, 18, 51, 52, 96, 123
Where to stay 59, 61
Wild dog 3, 21, 34, 50, 94, 108, 122
128, 177
Wildebeest 16, 19, 22, 24, 25, 86, 90, 93, 108, 122, 126, 147, 176
Wildlife Act of Parliament No 12 of 1998 123, 133
Wildlife and Environmental Conservation Society of Zambia (WECSZ) 87, 113
Wildlife checklist 144
Wildlife viewing loops 49, 83, 88, 95
133
Yellow baboon 123
Yellow-backed duiker 3, 22, 30, 73, 80, 128, 145, 176
Zambezi River 3, 4, 22, 73, 109
Zambia Tourism Board (ZTB) 16, 139
140
Zambia Wildlife Authority (ZAWA) 3, 4
50, 53, 56, 57, 58, 66, 69, 95, 115
120, 123, 124, 127, 128, 129, 133
135, 136, 139, 140
Zebra 16, 18, 19, 24, 52, 70, 85, 86
90, 93, 96, 108, 122, 147, 176

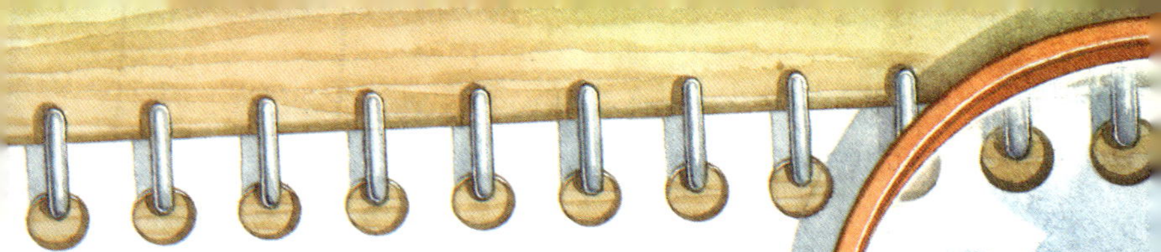

Pour chaque oiseau, plusieurs indices de reconnaissance sont indiqués. Lis-les bien tous, car c'est leur ensemble qui peut permettre une identification juste.
Tu trouveras donc :

● La **période de l'année**

J F M A M J J A S O N D

pendant laquelle l'espèce est visible en France est précisée par les carrés foncés, sauf si l'oiseau est présent toute l'année. Inutile en effet de croire avoir vu une hirondelle rustique au mois de janvier alors qu'elle ne revient d'Afrique qu'au mois d'avril !

● Le **régime alimentaire**, car il est souvent utile pour l'identification. Si tu observes un passereau avec une chenille dans le bec, il ne peut pas s'agir d'un granivore et inversement.

● Le **nom commun** en français.

Le rouge-queue à front blanc

J F M A M J J A S O N D

Insectes, vers, baies.

← 14 cm →

Très coloré, il se perche sur les basses branches et saute brusquement à terre pour attraper un ver ou une limace en hochant de la queue.

Tu trouveras également sur chaque double page des encadrés qui te permettront de comparer les espèces proches en vol et de découvrir leurs petites manies pour mieux les identifier.

● La **taille**, ← 14 cm → est indiquée en centimètres (cm). Elle correspond à la mesure de l'oiseau du bout du bec à l'extrémité de la queue et a surtout une valeur comparative par rapport aux espèces connues.

● **Un ou deux éléments** caractérisant l'oiseau : sa forme, son comportement ou son habitat. Si le chant de l'oiseau t'est indiqué, c'est qu'il est très facile à reconnaître en lisant la suite des lettres à haute voix.

Qu'est-ce qu'un oiseau ?

Tu sais reconnaître un rouge-gorge ou un merle noir parce que tu te souviens de leur silhouette et de leurs couleurs. Mais tu peux identifier bien d'autres espèces de la même façon, si tu mémorises les critères indispensables à leur détermination.

Les jumelles

Il est presque impossible d'observer attentivement un petit passereau sans jumelles, car il est souvent loin et toujours en mouvement. Choisis des jumelles 8 x 30 ou 10 x 40 qui correspondent a un bon compromis. En effet, 8 fois détermine la capacité de grossissement et 30 la luminosité des jumelles. Plus elles grossissent, plus il est difficile de viser la cible car le champ est faible. D'autre part, plus elles sont lumineuses et plus elles sont grosses et lourdes. À toi de choisir !

Le carnet de terrain

L'idéal est de prendre des notes sur un petit carnet de terrain, en faisant un dessin simple qui t'aidera à mémoriser tes observations.

Comment identifier un oiseau ?

Pour identifier un oiseau, il faut d'abord savoir l'observer et le décrire. Pose-toi plein de petites questions comme pour reconstituer un puzzle à partir de tes différentes observations :

La silhouette
Est-elle ronde (roitelet) ou élancée (bergeronnette) ? Quelle est la couleur des parties du corps (poitrine, ventre, dos...) ? L'oiseau a-t-il des taches ou des rayures sur le plumage ?

La taille
Essaye de l'évaluer par rapport à une espèce connue (plus grand ou plus petit qu'un moineau, un merle, un pigeon ou un canard).

La tête
Est-elle globuleuse (chouette) ou ronde (pigeon), dégagée du corps (tourterelle) ou rentrée dans les épaules (gros-bec) ? Regarde bien les dessins de la tête : calotte, sourcil, moustache... Quelle est la couleur de l'œil ? L'oiseau a-t-il une huppe (cochevis, huppe) ?

La queue
Est-elle longue (pie) ou courte (sittelle) ? Est-elle dressée (troglodyte) ? Quelle est la couleur du croupion ? Détermine sa forme.

carrée (étourneau) — *arrondie (corneille)* — *échancrée (chardonneret)* — *avec filets (hirondelle rustique)* — *fourchue (martinet)*

Le bec
Est-il court (mésange), fin (rouge-queue) ou fort (moineau), incurvé (grimpereau) ou crochu (faucon) ? Quelle est sa couleur ?

Les ailes
Sont-elles longues ou courtes, larges (pie) ou étroites (martinet), pointues (faucon) ou arrondies (geai) ? Le bout est-il digité (corbeau) ? De quelles couleurs sont-elles dessus et dessous ? Vois-tu des taches ou des barres alaires ?

Le vol
Est-il onduleux (pic, linotte) ou rectiligne (merle, moineau) ?

Les pattes
Sont-elles fines (pouillot) ou fortes (cygne) ? Sont-elles palmées (mouette), armées de griffes (chouette) ou emplumées (hibou) ? Quelle est leur couleur ?

La posture
Est-elle dressée (rouge-gorge), oblique (linotte), horizontale (bergeronnette) ou acrobatique (mésange) ?

Comment se déplace-t-il au sol ?
Marche-t-il (pigeon) ou sautille-t-il (moineau) ? Est-il perché ? Grimpe-t-il sur un tronc d'arbre (pic, grimpereau) ou descend-il la tête en bas (sittelle) ? Est-il toujours en vol (martinet) ou vole-t-il sur place (faucon crécerelle) ?

Pourquoi chantent-ils ?

Les mâles chantent au printemps, non pas parce qu'ils sont contents, mais pour attirer une femelle et signaler à leurs congénères qu'ici c'est chez eux. Ils se réservent ainsi un territoire d'alimentation et de reproduction pour assurer leur descendance.

Tout ronds, tout petits

Pfit... Tu as juste eu le temps d'apercevoir une petite boule de plumes et hop ! elle s'est faufilée sous un tas de bois ou entre les branches d'un sapin. Les plus petits de nos passereaux mesurent entre 8 et 11 cm. Ils sont difficiles à voir, mais ils chantent très fort et tu seras souvent étonné de découvrir le minuscule oiseau qui fait autant de bruit.

Le pouillot véloce ►

J F M A M J J A S O N D

Insectes. ←11 cm→

Tsip... tsap... tu entends le chant monotone de celui que l'on nomme le « compteur d'écus ». Tous les pouillots sont gris verdâtre avec un sourcil clair au-dessus de l'œil et un trait oculaire sombre.

Le troglodyte mignon ▼

Insectes. ←10 cm→

Il a un petit corps tout rond avec une queue dressée. Tic... tic... son cri cliquette, tandis qu'il sort et entre sans cesse d'un fourré ou d'un tas de bois.

Le pouillot fitis ▲

J F M A M J J A S O N D

Insectes et baies.

←11 cm→

Les notes flûtées de son chant mélancolique descendent en cascade. À l'automne, les jeunes ont le dessous entièrement jaune.

Le roitelet huppé ▼

Insectes ←9 cm→

C'est une petite boule qui virevolte sans arrêt dans les grands conifères sombres (ifs, sapins, épicéas), inspectant les rameaux à la recherche d'araignées et de petits insectes.

Le roitelet triple-bandeau ▼

Insectes. ←8 cm→

C'est le plus petit oiseau d'Europe. Il fréquente surtout les résineux, mais aussi les chênes verts et les cèdres dans le midi de la France.

Pattes à tout faire

Les oiseaux ont des pattes différentes selon leur mode de locomotion. Les percheurs ont un ongle postérieur recourbé qui rejoint les autres doigts et un système de verrouillage qui leur permet de dormir sans tomber (mésanges, roitelets). Les grimpeurs ont 2 doigts en avant et 2 en arrière (grimpereaux, pics). Les marcheurs ont un allongement de l'ongle postérieur pour augmenter la stabilité (bergeronnettes, cochevis).

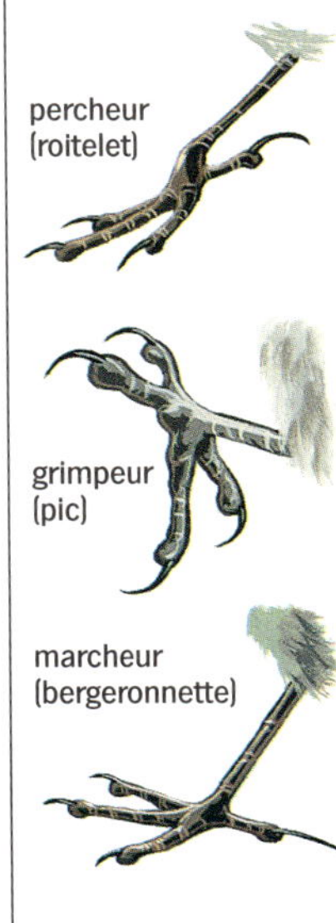

Les acrobates

Les mésanges sont les petits acrobates que tu vois se suspendre la tête en bas au bout des rameaux. Graines, chenilles ou larves d'insectes : tout est bon ! Plus petites qu'un moineau, elles sont assez colorées et virevoltent habilement sur ta mangeoire. Certaines d'entre elles peuvent nicher dans ta boîte aux lettres, d'autres préfèrent rester plus discrètes.

◄ La mésange bleue

Insectes. ←12 cm→
Plus petite, plus bleue et plus agile que la mésange charbonnière, elle n'a pas de « cravate noire » et se rencontre fréquemment dans les roselières.

La mésange noire ▲

Insectes, graines. ←11 cm→
Très vivace, elle virevolte dans les conifères. À l'automne, les populations du nord recherchent en bandes les graines d'épicéa pour faire des provisions.

La mésange huppée ▲

Insectes, graines. ←12 cm→
Gurrrr... tu entends un cri roulé dans un épicéa ou un pin ? C'est elle ! Elle ne fréquente que les conifères.

La mésange charbonnière

Insectes, baies et graines. ←13 cm→
Titidè... titidè... dès le mois de janvier, elle chante en répétant 2 ou 3 fois la même phrase. Très commune, on la voit souvent décortiquer les graines en tapant dessus avec son bec.

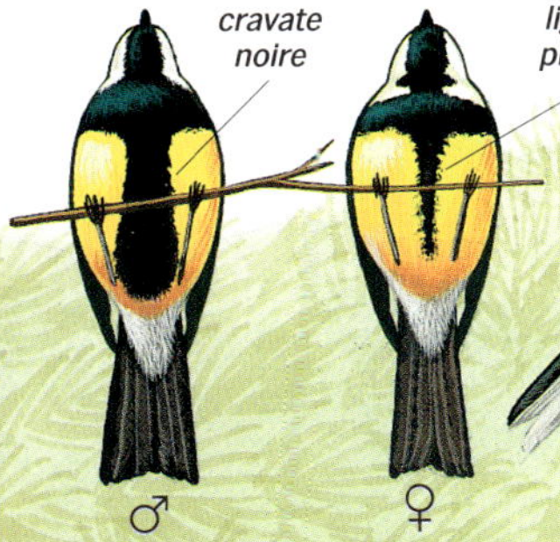

◄ La mésange nonnette

Insectes, graines.
←12 cm→
Elle décolle sans arrêt du sol, car elle recherche les insectes dans les herbes et les fourrés. L'hiver, elle picore les graines de chardons et de pissenlits.

À la mangeoire

Seules quelques espèces d'oiseaux sont attirées, l'hiver, par les graines de ta mangeoire :
la mésange charbonnière
et la mésange bleue,
le pinson des arbres,
le verdier, le gros-bec,
le moineau domestique,
le moineau friquet
et parfois le geai.
Tu peux ainsi réduire tes recherches d'identification !

La mésange à longue queue ►

Insectes. ←13 cm→
C'est une petite boule de plumes ébouriffée, piquée d'une longue queue. Elle se déplace en groupes familiaux en poussant de petits cris vifs : tsii, tsii, tsii...

D'un coup d'œil

bouvreuil

gros-bec

pinson des arbres

pinson du Nord

Les mangeurs de graines

Tu vois un groupe de petits passereaux qui grignotent des graines en volant d'arbre en arbre. Regarde leur bec : il est trapu et conique, typique des granivores. Certains vivent en bandes et causent souvent des dégâts (p. 10 et 11), d'autres sont solitaires (p. 12 et 13). La plupart recherchent leurs graines préférées dans les arbres ou près du sol. Regarde ce qu'ils mangent, cela t'aidera à les identifier.

Le sizerin flammé ►

Graines d'arbres, insectes.

←12 cm→

Ce petit oiseau rayé se suspend au bout des branches pour saisir des graines de bouleaux ou de pins. Il forme des troupes nombreuses l'hiver, quand les populations britanniques migrent chez nous.

Le chardonneret ◄ élégant

Graines, insectes.

←12 cm→

Il doit son nom à son attirance pour les graines de chardons, bardanes, centaurées, qu'il pille souvent à plusieurs. Il a la tête bigarrée et son vol est onduleux.

La linotte ◄ mélodieuse

Graines, insectes.
←13 cm→
Elle aime les terrains découverts parsemés de buissons (ajoncs, aubépines) et picore les graines, à terre ou dans la végétation basse. On la voit souvent en grands groupes pendant les migrations.

Le tarin ◄ des aulnes

Graines, baies.
←12 cm→
On le reconnaît à ses couleurs contrastées et à son bec, plus fin que celui des autres. Il se suspend facilement la tête en bas pour extraire les graines des aulnes.

Le gros-bec casse-noyaux ►

Graines, baies.
←18 cm→
Sa silhouette est massive et son bec énorme. Il s'en sert pour ouvrir les noyaux de cerises et de prunes et casser les graines de charmes et d'érables. C'est dans ces arbres que tu le verras.

En vol

serin cini

tarin

verdier

Le serin cini

Graines. ←11 cm→

C'est un tout petit passereau jaune à la silhouette ronde, qui picore les graines au sol. Il lance depuis son perchoir une sorte de grésillement, très aigu et rapide, qui sonne comme un grelot.

Le bruant zizi

Graines, insectes.

←16 cm→

Il se reconnaît au masque de la tête et à sa longue queue. L'hiver, il picore les graines de millet ou d'avoine ; l'été, il recherche les insectes dans les bois.

Le bruant jaune

Graines, baies. ←17 cm→
Il est souvent perché sur les fils électriques. Dans les champs, il picore les graines en sautillant au sol, accroupi sur ses pattes. La femelle a la tête plus jaune que celle du bruant zizi.

Emploi du temps

Chaque jour, les oiseaux respectent un emploi du temps rigoureux, qui dépend des conditions météo et des saisons. Pour satisfaire leur très grand besoin énergétique, ils mangent beaucoup, souvent, et transforment au plus vite les aliments en calories, sous peine de mort. Et s'ils passent du temps à leur toilette, c'est pour limiter les pertes caloriques. Parmi les petits oiseaux, seul le jeune martinet peut jeûner plusieurs jours.

Le bouvreuil pivoine

Graines, bourgeons, insectes.
←17 cm→
Souvent présent dans les arbres fruitiers, cet oiseau rondelet cause des dégâts : regarde-le cisailler les bourgeons floraux et écraser les graines !

Le pinson des arbres

Graines, insectes.
←15 cm→
Discrètement coloré, il vient sûrement l'hiver picorer en groupe à ta mangeoire. Il recherche les graines à terre et saisit quelques insectes au printemps pour ses petits.

Le pinson du Nord

J F M A M J J A S O N D

Graines, insectes.
←16 cm→
Hivernant chez nous, parfois en bandes immenses, il fréquente surtout les champs de maïs et les hêtraies car il raffole de leurs graines.

◀ Le moineau friquet

Graines, insectes.

← 14 cm →

Plus mobile que le moineau domestique, il est aussi plus discret et préfère la campagne à la ville. Chez cette espèce, les deux sexes sont semblables.

◀ Le verdier d'Europe

Graines, bourgeons.

← 14 cm →

Ce robuste passereau vert picore les céréales sans scrupules. Il ouvre aussi les samares des ormes et coupe les bourgeons et les jeunes pousses. Son chant est mélodieux.

Le moineau domestique

Omnivore.

← 15 cm →

Contrairement au moineau friquet, il n'a pas de tache noire sur les joues. Il est très commun en ville, où il mange de tout et forme la nuit des dortoirs bruyants.

Le rouge-gorge

Insectes, vers, baies.
←13 cm→
Tout rondelet et peu farouche, il sautille sur le sol en position dressée et quand il chante, il gonfle sa gorge rouge pour avoir l'air plus gros.

Les mangeurs d'insectes

Ils ont un bec fin et descendent volontiers au sol rechercher les insectes et les vers de terre. Écoute-les fouiner sous les feuilles et note leur façon de se déplacer, cela t'aidera à les identifier : plus ou moins gros, les percheurs sautillent, alors que les vrais marcheurs marchent ou courent.

L'accenteur mouchet

Insectes, graines.
←15 cm→
Très discret, il ne s'éloigne guère du couvert lorsqu'il pâture, en se déplaçant lentement au sol, le corps tassé sur ses pattes.

La ville : hôtel tout confort

De plus en plus d'oiseaux vivent en ville toute l'année. Ils y trouvent un gîte de première qualité (lampadaires, murs, toits, clochers...), à l'abri des prédateurs. La nourriture est abondante (insectes et déchets variés) et disponible à toute heure du fait de l'éclairage urbain qui prolonge la durée de chasse. Que rêver de mieux ?

Le cochevis huppé

Graines, insectes.

←17 cm→

Cette espèce d'alouette, dont le vol est onduleux, marche sur le bord des chemins en picorant des graines et des insectes, souvent dans le crottin des chevaux.

L'étourneau sansonnet

Omnivore

←18 cm→

Très bruyant, il marche ou court au sol et s'envole en bande pour rejoindre son dortoir. Ses cris sont rauques, mais il peut imiter le chant de nombreux oiseaux.

Le pic vert

Insectes, mollusques.

←31 cm→

De son vol onduleux, il quitte les troncs pour se poser dans un pré. Il se déplace par bonds et fouille la terre à la recherche de fourmis et d'escargots. Son cri est un éclat de rire sonore.

Le rossignol philomèle

J F M A M J J A S O N D

Insectes, baies.

←18 cm→

Toujours caché, il chante la nuit et au crépuscule pendant des heures. Ses phrases sont variées et entrecoupées de brefs silences.

Le merle noir

Vers, insectes, fruits. ←24 cm→

Très familier, il raffole des vers de terre qu'il attire en surface par ses sautillements et apprécie aussi les fruits. Souvent, il crie, très excité : tac, tac, tac...

La grive litorne

Vers, insectes, fruits.
←26 cm→
Toujours en groupe, elle picore les fruits mûrs des vergers ou sautille au sol. Comme toutes les grives, elle a la poitrine tachetée.

La grive draine

Vers, insectes, fruits. ←27 cm→
L'hiver, elle se nourrit de gui et en dissémine les graines. Elle chante souvent sous la pluie, en lançant de courtes phrases flûtées, séparées par des pauses nettes.

Horloge musicale

Au printemps, les oiseaux chantent dès l'aube ; mais chaque espèce, selon son rythme, commence à une heure précise. Note l'heure, cela t'aidera à les identifier.

6 h : rossignol (et alouette lulu).

6 h 30 : traquet tarier (et caille, merle).

7 h : rouge-gorge (et coucou, loriot).

7 h 30 : pinson (et pouillot véloce, mésange charbonnière).

8 h : pic vert (et geai, linotte).

◄ La grive musicienne

Vers, insectes, fruits.
←21 cm→
Tu vois un oiseau tacheté briser un escargot sur une pierre ? C'est elle. Elle chante à l'aube et au crépuscule en répétant toujours 3 ou 4 fois la même phrase.

Les hoche-queues

Sont regroupés ici les vrais hoche-queues (bergeronnettes) et les autres petits passereaux insectivores qui agitent, eux aussi, sans arrêt la queue (rouges-queues). Les premiers courent sur le sol, les autres repèrent leurs proies depuis un perchoir, mais quand tu les observes, tu es tout de suite frappé par ce mouvement incessant de la queue. Tu peux les différencier à leurs couleurs caractéristiques.

La bergeronnette grise

Insectes.

←20 cm→

Elle est noire et blanche et marche à petits pas pressés. Le long des talus et des flaques d'eau ou derrière le bétail, elle poursuit les insectes à terre ou en vol.

La bergeronnette des ruisseaux

Insectes, mollusques.

←21 cm→

Toujours active au bord de l'eau, elle attrape les larves et les libellules en volant sur place. Parfois, elle plonge le bec dans l'eau pour saisir un crustacé ou un petit poisson.

Le rouge-queue à front blanc

J F M A M J J A S O N D

Insectes, vers, baies.

←14 cm→

Très coloré, il se perche sur les basses branches et saute brusquement à terre pour attraper un ver ou une limace en hochant de la queue.

Le rouge-queue noir

Insectes, baies.

←15 cm→

Regarde bouger sa queue rousse ! Quittant son perchoir élevé, toujours à découvert, il capture ses proies en volant sur place ou parfois au sol.

Regarde-les voler !

Le merle : vol rectiligne.

Le pic vert : vol onduleux.

Selon les espèces, la trajectoire et le rythme des battements d'ailes sont différents. Le pigeon ramier a un vol battu, alors que la grive draine ferme ses ailes à intervalles réguliers. Les étourneaux, les merles et les moineaux suivent une ligne de vol rectiligne, alors que le chardonneret et le pic vert ondulent de haut en bas.

Œufs de Pâques !

Petit, gros, tacheté, vert ou rose, chaque espèce d'oiseaux pond des œufs différents. On les identifie à leur forme, leur taille, leur coloration et leur décoration (taches, points...). Attention ! ne les touche pas dans le nid, l'oiseau les abandonnerait.

elliptique

ovale

pointu

piriforme

Autres mangeurs d'insectes

Ils ont tous un bec fin, très pointu, adapté à la capture d'insectes et tu les observes toujours perchés dans les arbres ou les buissons. Les fauvettes ont une silhouette caractéristique, avec une gorge renflée qui leur fait une tête toute ronde et une queue arrondie au bout, plutôt longue. Sur les branches, elles ont une posture horizontale alors que le gobe-mouches se tient dressé.

Le gobe-mouches gris ▸

J F M A M J J A S O N D

Insectes, vers, baies.

← 14 cm →

Dressé sur son perchoir, il repère les insectes volants. Puis d'un coup d'aile, il les saisit en vol en claquant du bec et retourne se poser au même endroit.

La fauvette à tête noire

J F M A M J J A S O N D

Insectes, fruits. ← 14 cm →

Elle se distingue de la fauvette des jardins à sa calotte et de la fauvette mélanocéphale par l'absence de blanc sur le bord de la queue. Son chant mélodieux finit par des notes *forte*.

La fauvette grisette

J F M A M J J A S O N D

Insectes, baies.
← 14 cm →
Cette visiteuse d'été fréquente les milieux ouverts à végétation peu élevée : haies, prés, garrigues. C'est sur les buissons que le mâle chante, en hérissant ses plumes.

La fauvette des jardins ▼

J F M A M J J A S O N D

Insectes, baies. ← 14 cm →
Dans le sous-bois, à l'abri du feuillage, tu peux l'identifier par rapport aux autres, à sa livrée uniformément gris-beige, sans caractère saillant.

La fauvette ▲ mélanocéphale

Insectes, fruits, graines. ← 14 cm →
Visible uniquement dans la région méditerranéenne, elle est bruyante et circule sans arrêt dans les fourrés, près du sol. Inquiète, elle agite la queue ou l'étale.

◄ La fauvette babillarde

J F M A M J J A S O N D

Insectes, baies. ← 14 cm →
Cachée dans le maquis et les jeunes conifères, elle se distingue de la fauvette grisette par ses joues foncées et de la fauvette des jardins par ses rectrices externes blanches.

L'hirondelle rustique

J F M A M J J A S O N D

Insectes. ←19 cm→

On l'appelle aussi « hirondelle de cheminée ». À toute vitesse, elle rase les murs et les feuillages pour happer de minuscules insectes volants. Elle forme souvent des dortoirs dans les roselières. ▼

Les maîtres du vol

Ce sont les oiseaux que tu observes longuement en vol. Certains virevoltent à toute vitesse, en happant les insectes aériens (hirondelle, martinet), d'autres volent en faisant du surplace pour repérer

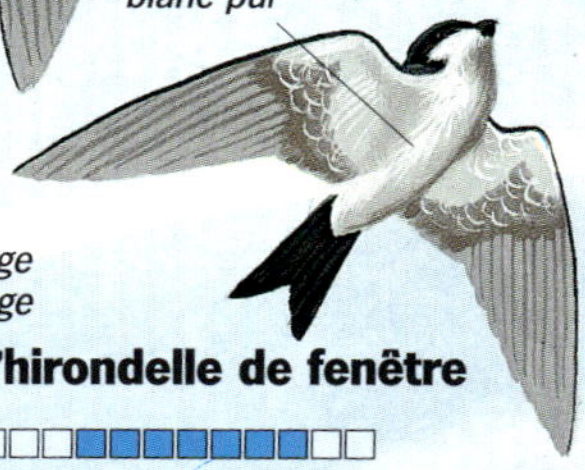

◄ L'hirondelle de fenêtre

J F M A M J J A S O N D

Insectes. ←13 cm→

Elle chasse assez haut dans le ciel et chante sur les fils électriques. Impossible de la confondre avec le martinet (sans tache au croupion), ni avec l'hirondelle rustique à la silhouette élancée.

Le martinet noir

J F M A M J J A S O N D

Insectes volants. ←16 cm→

Regarde son corps en forme de torpille et sa courte queue échancrée. Toujours en vol, même pour dormir, il alterne les petits battements d'ailes et les vol planés.

leurs proies (faucon). Leurs ailes, en forme de faux, sont adaptées à un vol rapide et précis et leur technique est remarquable. Suis-les des yeux, c'est vertigineux.

Le faucon crécerelle

Rongeurs, insectes.
←34 cm→
Tu vois souvent ce petit rapace faire « le Saint-Esprit » en volant sur place à plusieurs dizaines de mètres au-dessus d'un champ : il repère les rongeurs.

vol surplace

Chacun son nid

Les oiseaux utilisent à merveille tous les matériaux disponibles dans la nature.

La mésange à longue queue utilise des mousses et des toiles d'araignée. Elle garnit son nid de près de 2 000 plumes.

La sittelle rétrécit l'entrée de son trou par un mortier de terre finement posé, d'où son nom de torche-pot.

L'hirondelle construit une coupe avec des boulettes de boue et de salive, mélangées à des brins d'herbe.

Les grimpeurs

Petits ou gros oiseaux, ils grimpent en position verticale le long des troncs grâce à leurs pattes griffues. Avec leur long bec, fin ou puissant, ils recherchent des larves d'insectes xylophages ou des graines, tambourinent pour marquer leur territoire ou creusent une loge. Tous volent de tronc en tronc. Repère-les quand ils se posent.

❶ Le grimpereau des jardins

Insectes. ←12 cm→
Difficile à discerner avec sa couleur d'écorce, il grimpe en spirale le long des troncs par petits bonds et vole parfois en papillonnant.

❷ La sittelle torche-pot

Insectes, graines.
←14 cm→
Cette grimpeuse peut aussi descendre le long des troncs la tête en bas. Pour ouvrir les noisettes, elle les coince dans un trou d'écorce et les martèle à grands coups de bec : toc, toc, toc…

❸ Le pic épeichette

Insectes xylophages.

←14 cm→

Discret, ce tout petit pic escalade les branches fines en haut des arbres. Il tambourine plus longuement (une fois par seconde) et plus faiblement que les autres pics.

❹ Le pic épeiche

Graines, sève, œufs, insectes.

←22 cm→

De la taille d'un merle, ce pic soulève les écailles de pommes de pin pour saisir les graines. Il tambourine très vite (de 10 à 15 coups par seconde).

❺ Le torcol fourmilier

J F M A M J J A S O N D

Insectes. ←16 cm→

Discret dans ses habits couleur d'écorce, il est lent et a une remarquable mobilité du cou. Au moindre danger, il l'allonge et gonfle son plumage en soufflant.

Les pelotes

Les rapaces et les corvidés rejettent par le bec les parties non digérées des aliments (poils, os, restes d'insectes...). Tu peux ainsi trouver jusqu'à 100 pelotes de réjection d'un même rapace au pied d'un arbre. Leur forme et leur contenu sont caractéristiques de l'espèce.

Les rapaces nocturnes

Au crépuscule, tu distingues leurs gros yeux, dirigés vers l'avant et tu les vois s'envoler silencieusement. Les chouettes ont une allure toute ronde et les hiboux ont des aigrettes, mais tous ont des pattes plus ou moins emplumées, armées de griffes. Ils nichent dans des trous ou à l'intérieur d'habitations. Leur taille et leur ululement te permettront de les différencier.

Le hibou petit-duc ►

J F M A M J J A S O N D

Insectes ←19 cm→
Tout petit, on le voit parfois la nuit en ville chasser les insectes autour des lampadaires. Tiou... tiou... tiou... son chant entrecoupé de grands silences est répété à intervalles réguliers.

Le hibou moyen-duc ►

Rongeurs, oiseaux. ←35 cm→
Souvent présent dans les bois de conifères, il recherche, pour manger, les dortoirs de passereaux. Inquiet, il devient mince et droit comme un bâton.

La chouette chevêche

Insectes, rongeurs, oiseaux. ←21 cm→
Souvent visible le jour, perchée à découvert, elle chasse, à l'affût des campagnols ou des lézards. Au sol, elle sautille et avale des vers de terre.

La chouette hulotte ▼

Rongeurs, oiseaux.
←37 cm→
En vol, elle se distingue par son allure lourde et ses larges ailes arrondies. Dès qu'elle est dérangée, elle se jette sur tout prédateur menaçant sa nichée. Fais attention !

▲
La chouette effraie

Rongeurs, oiseaux.
←34 cm→
Au crépuscule, on la voit passer devant les phares des voitures et dans ton grenier, elle fait un raffut terrible avec ses soufflements et ses ronflements.

Tout gris, ils roucoulent !

Ils ont une petite tête et une longue queue et surtout, ils roucoulent. Certains ont envahi nos villes (pigeon biset), d'autres passent au-dessus des cols par centaines au moment des migrations (pigeon ramier, ou palombe, et tourterelle des bois). Tu trouves qu'ils se ressemblent tous, mais en les observant de plus près, essaye de les identifier.

Le pigeon biset de ville

Omnivore.
← 32 cm →
C'est celui qui arpente nos trottoirs et qui salit nos balcons. Ses couleurs sont très variables, mais son cou est souvent irisé de vert.

Le pigeon colombin

Graines, baies.
← 32 cm →
Il se distingue des autres par le fait qu'il n'a aucune marque blanche et niche dans les arbres creux.

Le pigeon ramier ▼

Graines, bourgeons, vers, insectes. ← 40 cm →
Il se dandine sur la pelouse en picorant le gazon et roucoule en 5 syllabes. À l'envol et à l'atterrissage, il claque des ailes et se déplace par grandes bandes, en septembre et en mars.

La tourterelle turque ▼

Graines. ← 27 cm →
Le vol saccadé des tourterelles les différencie des pigeons. Celle-ci, présente en France depuis 1950, profite des silos à maïs et apprécie les poulaillers.

Le pigeon voyageur

Depuis l'Antiquité, l'homme domestique le pigeon biset pour obtenir des sélections d'oiseaux aux silhouettes et coloris variés. Le pigeon voyageur est par exemple issu de ces modifications génétiques. Séparé de son conjoint, il est capable de parcourir 800 km pour regagner son pigeonnier à la vitesse de 80 km/h. De nombreuses sociétés colombophiles s'emploient, encore aujourd'hui, à améliorer la race.

La tourterelle des bois

J F M A M J J A S O N D

Graines. ← 27 cm →
◄ Très rousse par rapport à la tourterelle turque, elle est craintive et se repère au doux roucoulement des mâles, qui annonce les premières chaleurs de l'été.

Chacun son tour

Chez la plupart des espèces grégaires, les oiseaux profitent du groupe en suivant le mouvement, mais n'ont pas de relations entre eux. Par contre, chez les corbeaux freux, les choucas et les pigeons ramiers, chaque oiseau occupe une position sociale bien déterminée, qu'il défend au sein de la communauté. Ainsi, au moment des repas, les individus dominants mangent les premiers.

Les gros oiseaux noirs

Ils sont partout et tu les connais bien. Ce sont les corbeaux et les corneilles qui envahissent les décharges et picorent dans les champs, mais aussi les choucas et les pies voleuses. Certains sont bruyants et dérangent quand ils installent leur dortoir non loin de chez toi. Regarde-les bien, ils ont chacun des caractères distinctifs.

Le choucas ▸ des tours

Omnivore.
←32 cm→
Ce petit corvidé sociable a la tête ronde. Il picore au sol des limaces, des vers, des œufs et même des grenouilles et garde le contact avec ses congénères en criant en vol : tchiac...

La corneille noire

Omnivore.
←46 cm→
Plutôt solitaire, elle est très vigilante et repère de loin les nichées de passereaux qu'elle peut piller. Elle se nourrit aussi de cadavres ou de déchets.

Le corbeau freux

Mollusques, vers, insectes, graines. ←45 cm→
Il mange en groupe, il dort dans d'immenses dortoirs et il se reproduit en colonie. Au sol, il marche en se dandinant et fouille la terre de son bec puissant.

La pie bavarde

Omnivore. ←45 cm→
Se nourrissant, entre autres, de coléoptères et de papillons, elle est attirée par les couleurs métalliques et vole parfois des objets brillants. Écoute comme elle jacasse !

L'union fait la force

Certains oiseaux se rassemblent pour se reproduire (corbeaux freux), ou manger ensemble (chardonnerets, linottes). D'autres dorment en dortoir (étourneaux, moineaux, mésanges à longue queue) ou voyagent en bande (pinsons du Nord). Dans tous les cas, ce comportement grégaire est motivé par la recherche d'une plus grande sécurité. Les oiseaux peuvent profiter à plusieurs d'une bonne source de nourriture et affronter les prédateurs.

Les colonies de corbeaux ou « corbeautières » sont installées à la cime des grands arbres. Elles regroupent plusieurs centaines de couples qui reviennent chaque année.

Drôles de bains

Un oiseau se chauffe au soleil les ailes écartées ? C'est un rouge-gorge ou un étourneau. Ce dernier peut aussi se frotter les ailes avec des fourmis, alors que le geai et les grives s'accroupissent plutôt passivement sur une fourmilière. Quant au moineau, il préfère les bains de poussière.

Les oiseaux bizarres

Impossible de classer avec les autres ces gros oiseaux, dont l'allure étrange ou les couleurs très vives sont les signes les plus marquants. Ils n'ont rien de commun : l'un vole comme un papillon et dresse sa huppe en éventail quand il est inquiété (huppe) ; l'autre pille les fruits en ne laissant que la queue sur l'arbre (loriot) ; le troisième fait des réserves de glands pour l'hiver et oublie ses cachettes (geai).

La huppe fasciée

Insectes. ← 27 cm →
Hochant de la tête, elle trottine rapidement au sol à la recherche d'insectes, puis les jette en l'air avant de les avaler. En vol, elle ressemble à un gros papillon.

Le loriot d'Europe

J F M A M J J A S O N D

Insectes, fruits.
←23 cm→
Malgré sa couleur vive, il reste bien camouflé en haut des arbres, car il est très farouche. On découvre plutôt ses méfaits après son passage sur les cerisiers, les abricotiers et les figuiers...

Le geai des chênes

Glands, fruits, insectes.
←33 cm→
Souvent en groupe au début du printemps, il lance son cri rauque et désagréable : schrack... À l'automne, il fait des réserves de glands qu'il cache dans des fentes d'arbres ou dans le sol.

Partir ou non !

Même les petits passereaux migrent jusqu'en Afrique s'ils ne trouvent pas une nourriture suffisante là où ils nichent. Certaines migrations sont « totales » : ainsi tous les rossignols partent au printemps vers le sud. D'autres sont dites « partielles » si seulement une partie des individus migrent. L'hiver, on voit ainsi ensemble des oiseaux qui vivent chez nous toute l'année (rouge-gorge sédentaire) et des sujets venus du nord hiverner en France.

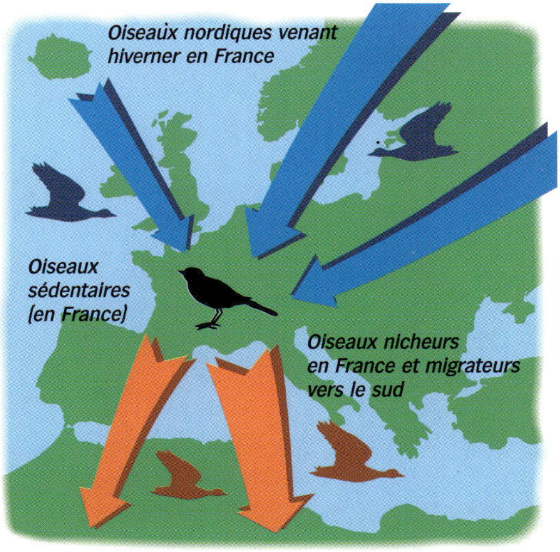

Calendrier d'observation des oiseaux

Chaque mois, il se passe quelque chose de nouveau du côté des petits oiseaux. Profites-en pour ouvrir l'œil :

JANVIER :
les corbeaux freux et les choucas se rassemblent en petits groupes pour se nourrir et les grives se gavent de gui.

FÉVRIER :
les premières hirondelles sont visibles dans le Midi et déjà, l'accenteur mouchet commence à chanter.

MARS :
arrivée des hirondelles rustiques et de rivage, puis de la huppe fasciée. À la fin du mois, tu entends le pouillot fitis et les premiers rossignols philomèles.

AVRIL :
quelques pinsons du Nord s'attardent encore. Les rossignols arrivent en groupes au milieu du mois et les hirondelles atteignent maintenant le reste de la France. Vers le 20, tu peux aussi guetter les premiers martinets noirs.

MAI :
la migration bat son plein. On voit passer les tourterelles des bois, quand elles ne sont pas abattues lors des chasses à la palombe, dans le Médoc.

Juin :
la reproduction a déjà commencé ou est même achevée pour beaucoup d'oiseaux. Les chants font place aux cris des jeunes qui quémandent la becquée.

Juillet :
c'est un mois difficile pour les débutants en ornithologie, car les oiseaux sont en mue et le plumage des jeunes n'est pas facile à reconnaître.
Les martinets se préparent déjà au départ.

Août, septembre, octobre :
départ en migration de tous les limicoles, c'est-à-dire les oiseaux d'eau douce aux longues pattes qui survolent la campagne, même s'ils ne se posent pas dans ton jardin. Tu peux aller te poster sur un col migratoire pour observer le passage des fringilles et de quelques rouges-gorges.
La nuit, on entend passer les grives musiciennes dont les cris en migration sont caractéristiques. Les fauvettes à tête noire et les pouillots véloces quittent le Nord pour venir hiverner chez nous.

Novembre, décembre :
c'est le début de l'hiver, tu peux commencer à observer les visiteurs de ta mangeoire : mésanges charbonnières et bleues, pinsons, verdiers...

Index

a

Accenteur mouchet, *Prunella modularis* ☐ 16

b

Bergeronnette des ruisseaux, *Motacilla cinerea* ☐ 20
Bergeronnette grise, *Motacilla alba* ☐ 20
Bouvreuil pivoine, *Pyrrhula pyrrhula* ☐ 13
Bruant jaune, *Emberiza citrinella* ☐ 13
Bruant zizi, *Emberiza cirlus* ☐ 12

c

Chardonneret élégant, *Carduelis carduelis* ☐ 10
Choucas des tours, *Corvus monedula* ☐ 32
Chouette chevêche, *Athene noctua* ☐ 29
Chouette effraie, *Tyto alba* ☐ 29
Chouette hulotte, *Strix aluco* ☐ 29
Cochevis huppé, *Galerida cristata* ☐ 17
Corbeau freux, *Corvus frugilegus* ☐ 33
Corneille noire, *Corvus corone corone* ☐ 32

e

Étourneau sansonnet, *Sturnus vulgaris* ☐ 17

f

Faucon crécerelle, *Falco tinnunculus* ☐ 25
Fauvette à tête noire, *Sylvia atricapilla* ☐ 22
Fauvette babillarde, *Sylvia curruca* ☐ 23
Fauvette des jardins, *Sylvia borin* ☐ 23
Fauvette grisette, *Sylvia communis* ☐ 23
Fauvette mélanocéphale, *Sylvia melanocephala* ☐ 23

g

Geai des chênes, *Garrulus glandarius* ☐ 35
Gobe-mouches gris, *Muscicapa striata* ☐ 22
Grimpereau des jardins, *Certhia brachydactyla* ☐ 26-27
Grive draine, *Turdus viscivorus* ☐ 19
Grive litorne, *Turdus pilaris* ☐ 19
Grive musicienne, *Turdus philomelos* ☐ 19
Gros-bec casse-noyaux, *Coccothraustes coccothraustes* ☐ 11

h

Hibou moyen-duc, *Asio otus* ☐ 28
Hibou petit-duc, *Otus scops* ☐ 28
Hirondelle de cheminée, *Hirundo rustica* ☐ 24
Hirondelle de fenêtre, *Delichon urbica* ☐ 24
Hirondelle rustique : *voir hirondelle de cheminée*
Huppe fasciée, *Upupa epops* ☐ 34

l

Linotte mélodieuse, *Carduelis cannabina* ☐ 11
Loriot d'Europe, *Oriolus oriolus* ☐ 35

m

Martinet noir, *Apus apus* ☐ 24
Merle noir, *Turdus merula* ☐ 18
Mésange à longue queue, *Aegithalos caudatus* ☐ 9
Mésange bleue, *Parus Caeruleus* ☐ 8
Mésange charbonnière, *Parus major* ☐ 9
Mésange huppée, *Parus cristatus* ☐ 8
Mésange noire, *Parus ater* ☐ 8
Mésange nonnette, *Parus palustris* ☐ 9
Moineau domestique, *Passer domesticus* ☐ 15
Moineau friquet, *Passer montanus* ☐ 15

p

Pic épeiche, *Dendrocopos major* ☐ 26-27
Pic épeichette, *Dendrocopos minor* ☐ 26-27
Pic vert, *Picus viridis* ☐ 17
Pie bavarde, *Pica pica* ☐ 33
Pigeon biset, *Columba livia* ☐ 30
Pigeon colombin, *Columba œnas* ☐ 30
Pigeon ramier, *Columba palumbus* ☐ 31
Pinson des arbres, *Fringilla cœlebs* ☐ 14
Pinson du Nord, *Fringilla montifringilla* ☐ 14
Pouillot fitis, *Phylloscopus trochilus* ☐ 6
Pouillot véloce, *Phylloscopus collybita* ☐ 6

r

Roitelet huppé, *Regulus regulus* ☐ 7
Roitelet triple-bandeau, *Regulus ignicapillus* ☐ 7
Rossignol philomèle, *Luscinia megarhynchos* ☐ 18
Rouge-gorge, *Erithacus rubecula* ☐ 16
Rouge-queue à front blanc, *Phœnicurus phœnicurus* ☐ 21
Rouge-queue noir, *Phœnicurus ochruros* ☐ 21

s

Serin cini, *Carduelis serinus* ☐ 12
Sittelle torchepot, *Sitta europaea* ☐ 26-27
Sizerin flammé, *Carduelis flammea* ☐ 10

t

Tarin des aulnes, *Carduelis spinus* ☐ 11
Torcol fourmilier, *Jynx torquilla* ☐ 26-27
Tourterelle des bois, *Streptopelia turtur* ☐ 31
Tourterelle turque, *Streptopelia decaocto* ☐ 31
Troglodyte mignon, *Troglodytes troglodytes* ☐ 6

v

Verdier d'Europe, *Carduelis chloris* ☐ 15

Lorsque tu as identifié un oiseau, coche le ☐ correspondant à son nom.

Loi 49.956 du 16.07.1949
Dépôt légal : 2e trimestre 1997
ISBN : 2.84113.144.0
Imprimé en Italie
par G. Canale & C. S.p.A., Borgaro T.se, Turin.